WHY SUICIDE?

Other Books by Eric Marcus

The Male Couple's Guide

*Making History: The Struggle for Gay
and Lesbian Equal Rights, 1945–1990*

Expect the Worst (You Won't Be Disappointed)

Is It a Choice?

Breaking the Surface

WHY

SUICIDE?

Answers to 200 of

the Most Frequently

Asked Questions

About Suicide,

Attempted Suicide,

and Assisted Suicide

ERIC MARCUS

HarperSanFrancisco
An Imprint of HarperCollinsPublishers

HarperCollins®, 🏭 ®, and HarperSanFrancisco™ are trademarks of HarperCollins Publishers Inc.

HarperCollins Web Site: http://www.harpercollins.com

FIRST EDITION

Library of Congress Cataloging-in-Publication Data

Marcus, Eric.
   Why suicide? : answers to 200 of the most frequently asked questions about suicide, attempted suicide, and assisted suicide / Eric Marcus.
ISBN 0–06–251166–1 (pbk.)

1. Suicide 2. Suicide—Prevention. 3. Assisted suicide. I. Title.

HV6545.M256   1996
362.2'8—dc20

95-33431

06 07 08 09❖ RRD(H) 20 19 18 17 16 15 14 13

To my father

and to Dr. Stephen Frommer,
who helped me reclaim him

CONTENTS

SPECIAL
ACKNOWLEDGMENTS

I am especially grateful to Jennifer M. Finlay, who searched high and low for information on every possible aspect of suicide. Her curiosity and thoroughness added enormously to this book, and her sense of humor was indispensable. A special thanks also to Linda Alband and Linda M. Finlay.

Though Jennifer and I drew material from scores of resources, George Howe Colt's *The Enigma of Suicide* was invaluable. Colt covers all aspects of this issue with unparalleled clarity and thoroughness. I am extremely grateful for his work, and you will see footnote references to his book throughout this one. I highly recommend *The Enigma of Suicide* to anyone who wishes to explore further the issue of suicide.

ACKNOWLEDGMENTS

Many thanks to my editor Barbara Moulton for helping shape the idea for *Why Suicide?* and for believing in this project. Thank you to my agent, Jed Mattes, for helping me place this book, at long last. As always, my thanks to associate editor Lisa Bach. Thanks to copyeditor Carl Walesa for his meticulous work. Thank you also to all those who shared their stories, suggested questions, offered sage advice, and/or read all or part of the manuscript, especially my friends Kate Chieco and Benjamin Dreyer. I could not have completed this book without you.

And a very big thank you to my family and friends for their support during what turned out to be a long and arduous project. These include Mark Burstein, Posy Gering, Cecilia Marcus, May Marcus, Brett Morrow, Phil Roselin, and Stuart Schear. A very special thank you to Barney Karpfinger, for a lot.

INTRODUCTION

Almost all of us are touched at some point in life by suicide, whether it's the suicide or attempted suicide of someone we know, our own passing thoughts of suicide, or a heartfelt plea from a terminally ill loved one who wishes a swift and painless end to life.

No matter what the circumstances, there are always questions for those of us who are affected. Perhaps the most perplexing and difficult to answer is, Why? But that's only the first of scores of questions. When I was twelve, my own father committed suicide. I had lots of questions, but there was no one who could provide the answers. The adults in my life, it turns out, didn't have answers to give. They didn't even know where to turn for help.

That's why I've written *Why Suicide?* It's the book I wish my family could have read when I was a child, so they could have helped me get through the trauma of my father's death. It's the book I wish I could have consulted when a terminally ill friend asked me to help him die with dignity, so I could have fully understood the implications of what he was asking me to do. And it's the book that has, at long last, provided me with answers to many of the questions about suicide that I've carried for the past twenty-five years.

I hope the questions and answers in *Why Suicide?* bring understanding and comfort to all of you who are in some way touched by suicide.

I don't pretend to be an expert on the subject of suicide, which is why I talked to plenty of other people (including many experts), depended on magazine and newspaper articles, and scanned the pages of many, many books. In my research, I had the extensive help of Jennifer Finlay, an experienced researcher who worked with journalist Randy Shilts on his monumental work about gays in the military, *Conduct Unbecoming.*

What Jennifer and I learned about suicide you'll find in the pages that follow, including all kinds of questions, from the very basic to the extremely specific. In response to these questions you'll find brief answers, long answers, anecdotes, opinion, and conjecture. A few of the questions will leave you with more questions, because I've included some that don't yet have definitive answers.

You'll meet many different people in *Why Suicide?* Some give answers to questions; others provide stories that help support a point of view. When I've used quotes or anecdotes from experts and those whose stories have been made public, I have used complete names. When I've quoted private citizens or used their anecdotes—or composites drawn from several different people—I've used only first names and altered identifying characteristics to protect the privacy of the people I'm quoting.

Why Suicide? includes more than two hundred questions; but not all the possible questions are here, nor are all the answers. If there's a question I've missed that you'd like answered, or if you have an answer to a question that I didn't have an answer for or that you feel I didn't answer adequately, write to me in care of my publisher.

Eric Marcus
c/o Harper San Francisco
1160 Battery Street
San Francisco, CA 94111

CHAPTER 1

THE BASICS

Who? What? Where? When? Why?

W*hat is suicide?*

At its simplest, suicide is the act of killing oneself on purpose. The word *suicide* comes from the Latin *sui*, meaning "self," and *caedere*, which means "to kill." But this definition is deceptively simple, because in reality suicide is many things to different people: tragic, shocking, horrifying, enraging, mysterious, a relief, a shame, a stigma, a shattering legacy, a cry for help, a release from pain, selfish, heroic, insane, a way out, the right choice, the last word, punishment, revenge, a protest, a weapon, a political statement,

1

tempting, desperate, upsetting, unsettling, a mistake, angry, hurtful, dramatic, a cop-out, devastating, and unforgivable.

In the pages and chapters that follow, you'll see how the act of taking one's life can be so many things, and more.

○ **What about someone who drinks himself to death? Is that suicide?**

It's not exactly like shooting yourself or swallowing a fatal dose of pills, but the results are the same. Some people call this type of suicide *indirect suicide* or *slow suicide*. Other forms of behavior that could be considered indirect suicide or slow suicide include knowingly engaging in sexual behavior that will expose you to HIV, continuing to smoke if you have emphysema, and eating sweets if you have diabetes.

○ **Is it considered a form of suicide to refuse medical treatment?**

Some people consider this a form of indirect suicide, but it really depends upon the circumstances. For someone who has a treatable but potentially fatal condition, refusing medical treatment is a decision that many would view as suicidal. But for someone who is in the end stages of a terminal disease, refusing treatment may very well be a rational, appropriate choice, especially if treatment will simply extend life and not improve it or even maintain its quality.

○ **How many people commit suicide in the United States?**

The official number is approximately thirty thousand people a year, but the real figure may be as high as three to five times that number because many (if not most) suicides go unreported.

Statisticians also speak in terms of the *suicide rate*. By this, they mean the number of people per 100,000 who take their lives. On average, the annual suicide rate of all Americans is about 12 per 100,000 people.

In 1993, suicide was the ninth leading cause of death in the United States, behind HIV, which killed 38,500 people, and ahead of homicide, which took 25,470 lives.

○ *Why are so many suicides not reported?*

Doctors, medical examiners, and coroners have long spared families the added grief, stigma, and shame of having suicide listed as the official cause of death.

In my father's case, his official cause of death was pneumonia. Technically, this was true. But it was also true that the pneumonia was a result of an overdose of a prescription medication. Because the true cause of death was not listed, my family didn't have to deal with the public stigma and shame of my father's suicide, at least as long as no one talked about the true cause of death.

Denial also plays a part in the underreporting. For some families, denial may lead to the belief that their loved one's death was accidental, whether that person took an overdose of pills, shot himself or herself, or intentionally drove into a highway overpass at high speed. And the medical examiner or coroner may be willing to go along with the family's denial in order to spare them from having to confront the truth.

○ *Do life-insurance issues have anything to do with why people don't want suicide to be listed as the official cause of death?*

Many of the people I talked to in the course of researching this book were under the mistaken assumption that when someone commits suicide, that person's life-insurance policy is automatically voided. As long as the policy has been in effect for more than two years, full benefits will in fact be paid.

In general, according to Bernard Granville, who has been an insurance broker in New York City for thirty years, if someone commits suicide within two years of the date a policy becomes effective, the amount received by the beneficiary will be limited to the premiums paid in, plus interest. But after two years, the policy is incontestable; in other words, the policy will be paid.

○ *Is the rate of suicide in the United States the same as it was years ago?*

The suicide rate today, about 12 per 100,000, is a little higher than it was at the turn of the century, when the rate was around 10 per 100,000. During the years in between, the rate fluctuated depending upon economic conditions and whether the country was at war. During times of economic hardship the suicide rate went up, as it did during the Depression, reaching a high of 17.4 in 1932. During the two world wars, as "personal woes [were] overshadowed by the larger conflict," the rate went down. For example, "during World War I the rate dipped from 16.2 in 1915 to 11.5 in 1919. . . . During World War II the rate sank to a low of 10.0." (Colt, *The Enigma of Suicide*, p. 247)

○ *How many people attempt suicide?*

Although there are no official domestic or international statistics on the number of attempted suicides, the American Association of Suicidology estimates that there are at least eight to twenty attempts for each death from suicide. So if we accept the official figure of 30,000 deaths from suicide in the United States each year, we can extrapolate that there are from 240,000 to 600,000 attempted suicides each year in the United States.

For young people, researchers estimate that there are two hundred attempts for every completed suicide. By comparison, among the elderly, there are only four attempts for every completed suicide. For more information on these subjects, see chapter 3, "Teen/Youth Suicide"; chapter 4, "Suicide and the Elderly"; and chapter 5, "Attempted Suicide."

○ *Is suicide against the law?*

The specific laws regarding suicide vary by state, but whatever the variations, people who attempt or commit suicide are not punished under the law in the United States.

For example, as noted in the 1985 *Duquesne Law Review*, in New Jersey, the state with the lowest suicide rate, the state legislature in 1972 repealed the state law that classified suicide as a disorderly offense and enacted the following sections:

> 1. Any person who attempts to commit suicide shall not be guilty of a criminal offense, and such attempt shall not be an indictable offense.
> 2. Any person who attempts to commit suicide shall fall under the jurisdiction of the involuntary commitment and subject to temporary hospitalization as provided herein.

Nevada, the state with the highest rate of suicide, about twice the national average, had laws on the books until the mid-1960s that made suicide a criminal offense. According to the *Duquesne Law Review*, the Nevada legislature first specifically and comprehensively addressed suicide in 1911 legislation that provided:

SEC. 114 Suicide is the intentional taking of one's own life.

SEC. 115 Every person who, with intent to take his own life, shall commit upon himself any act dangerous to human life, or which, if committed upon or toward another person and followed by death as a consequence, would render the perpetrator chargeable with homicide, shall be punished by imprisonment in the state penitentiary for not more than two years, or by a fine of not more than one thousand dollars.

SEC. 116 Every person who, in any manner, shall willfully advise, encourage, abet or assist another in taking his own life shall be guilty of manslaughter.

SEC. 117 Every person who, in any manner, shall willfully advise, encourage, abet, or assist another person in attempting to take the latter's life shall be punished by imprisonment in the state penitentiary for not more than ten years.

SEC. 118 The fact that the person attempting to take his own life was incapable of committing crime shall not be a defense to a prosecution under either of sections 116 or 117 of this act.

As the *Duquesne Law Review* stated, "Sections 114 and 115 were repealed two years later. The other three sections remained the law until they were repealed in 1967. In the interim, an act was passed in 1957, providing a criminal penalty for '[e]very person who shall willfully attempt to take his life by any means whatsoever.' This act was repealed in 1966."

○ *What about assisted suicide? Is it against the law to help someone kill himself?*

Yes, although the specific laws vary from state to state. In general, these laws say that it is a crime for one person to intentionally aid someone else in committing suicide. For more information on this subject, see chapter 8, "Assisted Suicide."

○ *Is suicide a sin?*

This is one of those subjective questions whose answer is in the eye of the beholder. Personally, I think suicide is a lot of things, but I don't think it's a sin. If, however, your religious convictions lead you to believe that only God can give life and therefore only God can take it, then you're likely to believe committing suicide is breaking God's law and is therefore a sinful act.

○ *What does the Bible say about suicide?*

I always assumed that the Bible both condemned and prohibited suicide. But I was wrong. As George Howe Colt states in his book *The Enigma of Suicide,* "Considering Christianity's nearly two thousand years of intense opposition to suicide, it is surprising that neither the Old nor the New Testament directly prohibits the act." The Old and New Testaments combined tell only a handful of stories about suicide, and those are told without judgment one way or the other.

○ *What are Jewish and Christian attitudes toward suicide? Is it considered sinful?*

Traditional Christian doctrine has for centuries judged suicide to be a mortal sin. But as Rita Robinson explains in her book *Survivors of Suicide,* "Most religious communities, while not condoning suicide, empathize with the deceased and offer love and compassion to the survivors." She goes on to note that this wasn't always the case and that only a quarter century ago the Catholic Church, for example, considered suicide a public scandal and forbade burial within the church.

Joanne, a devout Catholic who lost her teenage son to suicide four years ago, assumed that her church would take a harsh view toward his suicide. "From what I learned when I was growing up, committing suicide was a mortal sin, so you can imagine how that made me feel. It was awful enough to lose my child, and in that way, but the burden of knowing that he couldn't have a church funeral tore me up." Joanne's worst fear was never realized. "The day after Kevin died, my priest came to see me at home and he was wonderful. He told me that Kevin wasn't in his right mind when he did this and for that reason what he did was not a sin." Kevin's funeral was officiated by the priest at the family's church.

In Judaism, as Isaac Klein explains in A *Guide to Jewish Religious Practice*, "the rabbis ruled that no [mourning] rites whatsoever should be observed for a suicide. . . . Suicide was considered a moral wrong. Deliberate destruction of one's own life was rebellion against God." That said, Klein goes on to explain that virtually all suicides are not actually considered suicides, based on rabbinical interpretation of what in fact constitutes a suicide. As he explains, "The only suicide for whom mourning is not observed is one who killed himself out of a cynical disregard for life; this excludes one who killed himself because he could not cope with his problems." Klein continues: "Nowadays, since it is known that most cases of suicide result from temporary insanity caused by depression, we observe all the rites of mourning."

○ *Does the person who commits suicide go to hell?*

To me, it felt like a living hell when my father committed suicide. But as far as where my father went after he died, I thought he suffered plenty while he was alive, so I always imagined he was in heaven.

Not everyone takes such a benign view. If you adhere to traditional religious beliefs, depending upon your religion, those who commit suicide may wind up in hell. For example, when it comes to Islam, as noted in the *Encyclopedia of Religion*, "Muhammad proclaimed that a person who commits suicide will be denied Paradise and will spend his time in Hell repeating the deed by which he has ended his life."

○ *Does everyone have thoughts of suicide?*

Most people have had casual thoughts of suicide at one time or another, especially when faced with life's frustrations and disappointments. This is perfectly normal, although if the thoughts are more than casual and don't pass quickly, there is reason to be concerned. Please see chapter 6, "Treatment and Prevention," for a series of questions about what to do if you're feeling suicidal.

○ *Do suicidal feelings pass?*

In most cases, yes. People who have casual or even less than casual suicidal feelings will eventually get over them. But there is much more involved in answering this question. Please see chapter 6, "Treatment and Prevention," for a complete answer.

○ *Can you tell if someone is feeling suicidal?*

Often, you can tell. Most people who are feeling suicidal give clues that something is wrong. For a detailed answer to this question and a list of possible warning signs, see chapter 6, "Treatment and Prevention."

○ *What are some of the most common myths about suicide?*

There are many, and I list some of them here. I've drawn this list from several sources, including a list first prepared in 1961 by Edwin S. Shneidman called "Facts and Fables on Suicide" and the chapter titled "Suicide Myths" in Rita Robinson's book *Survivors of Suicide*.

People who talk about killing themselves won't do it.
Wrong. People who talk about wanting to die need to be taken seriously, because some people who talk about it do it.

There are no warning signs.
According to Edwin Shneidman, "Of any ten persons who kill themselves, eight have given definite warnings of their suicidal intentions."

Young people are more likely than old people to kill themselves.
People sixty-five and older kill themselves at a higher rate than those aged fifteen to twenty-four.

Bad weather drives up suicide rates.
Spring is the time of year when people commit suicide in the greatest numbers.

People who make one attempt will never try it again.
Most people who attempt suicide will never try it again. But 10 percent of those who attempt suicide once will eventually take their own lives.

Suicide is against the law.
It's not, but if you're caught assisting in a suicide, you can be charged with a criminal offense in all fifty states.

Most people leave suicide notes.
They don't. Only one in five or six people who commit suicide leaves a note.

People who are suicidal want to die.
Not necessarily. Most people who are suicidal are ambivalent. And some of those who are consciously using suicide as a cry for help or a threat accidentally wind up dead.

Suicide is genetic.
Though there is no "suicide gene," there *are*, as Rita Robinson notes, "sociological and biological factors in families that might seem to dispose them to suicide." For example, you're several times more likely to commit suicide if you come from a family where someone has killed himself. Though the reason isn't entirely clear, part of it has to do with the example set by that relative and part of it may have to do with inherited characteristics ranging from depression to dark temperament.

Poor people are more likely to kill themselves.
       or
Rich people are more likely to kill themselves.
As several experts have said to me, "Suicide is an equal-opportunity killer."

Once a suicidal crisis has passed, the person is out of danger.
As Edwin Shneidman explains, "Most suicides occur within about three months following the beginning of improvement, when the individual has the energy to put his morbid thoughts and feelings into effect."

○ **Do people plan their suicides?**

Many people who commit suicide do so on impulse and make no significant plans in advance. This is, perhaps, part of the reason only one in five or six people who commit suicide leaves a note. Others do plan their suicides, making preparations over a period of days, weeks, or months.

Ruth was in her eighties, and had recently been incapacitated by a fall, when she first started thinking about ending her life. "I wasn't in any kind of a rush, but I've always been very organized about things. So I made a list of all the things I needed to do, from finding out exactly how I was going to do it, to saving up the right pills, to making sure all of my papers were in order, to giving away some things that I'd been saving for various people." Ruth spent several months preparing for her suicide before actually following through with her plan. In chapter 4, "Suicide and the Elderly," and in chapter 5, "Attempted Suicide," Ruth talks at greater length about her experience.

○ *Do animals other than humans commit suicide? Why?*

Because it's impossible to interview animals other than humans about suicide, it's difficult to know for sure if what appears to be suicidal behavior is in fact suicidal behavior. But there are cases that look like the real thing. As explained by reporter Natalie Angier in a *New York Times* article dated April 5, 1994, "Biologists have identified numerous examples of creatures that sacrifice themselves for their kin, from termites that explode their guts, releasing the slimy, foul contents over enemies that threaten their nest, to rodents that deliberately starve themselves to death rather than risk spreading an infection to others in their burrow."

Then there's the issue of depression, which apparently isn't restricted only to humans. Kathy, the dolphin who played the title role in the 1960s television show *Flipper*, was moved to a small steel tank following the cancellation of her show, where she had little contact with people. Her trainer, Richard O'Barry, related the story of her death in his arms in a January

1993 article in *Smithsonian* magazine. "[She] committed suicide. I don't know what else to call it; it was deliberate. Every breath is a conscious effort for a dolphin, and she just stopped breathing. She died of a broken heart."

Another story, one that I found particularly compelling, was told in a *San Francisco Examiner* article dated April 13, 1994. Octavia, a fifty-eight-pound octopus, lived in captivity in the Cabrillo Marine Museum in San Pedro, California. With tentacles measuring twelve feet in length, she didn't have a lot of room to stretch out in her four-foot-deep, six-foot-by-six-foot tank. On a Sunday night when no one was at the museum, she lifted a drainpipe two inches in diameter out of its fitting, and the water drained out. She was found dead the next morning.

Perhaps lemmings are best known for what appears to be their suicidal behavior. The lemming is a furry-footed, six-inch-long rodent that lives in northern climates. Every four years lemmings migrate en masse in search of adequate sources of food to feed their growing numbers. Apparently they go off in a random direction, one following the other, in a straight line. No matter what the obstacle, they don't alter their migratory course, which can be suicidal, especially if a cliff or a large body of water gets in the way.

○ *What is suicidology?*

Suicidology is the study of suicide and its prevention. The word was coined by Edwin Shneidman, who along with Norman L. Farberow conducted pioneering research in the 1950s and 1960s on the subject of suicide that challenged long-held assumptions.

○ *Who commits suicide?*

Fathers, mothers, grandparents, children, siblings, friends, rich people, poor people, famous actors, big-city policemen, straight athletes, gay teens, old people, young people, black people, Hispanics, whites, Native Americans, schizophrenics and manic depressives, alcoholics, the clean and sober, healthy people, terminally ill people, those from stable families where there's never been a suicide, and those whose families are hopelessly fractured. No group is exempt no matter how you slice the human family pie. That said, people from some groups commit suicide in greater numbers than do people from others. In the questions that follow, I'll take a look at some specific groups and how their risk of suicide differs from the norm. I'll also try to tell you why, but that isn't always as clear as the numbers.

○ *Who is most likely to commit suicide?*

White men aged sixty-five and older are the most likely to commit suicide. But in general, those more likely to commit suicide are older and male, tend to be isolated, suffer from some kind of mental illness such as depression or schizophrenia, and have drug and/or alcohol problems.

○ *Why white men aged sixty-five and older?*

At first glance, you would think that in comparison to any other segment of the population over sixty-five, white men would be in the best position and therefore the least likely to commit suicide. When it comes to economic status, they are indeed in the best position. But after they turn sixty-five, white men experience considerable loss in terms of their jobs, status, and health. All segments of the over-sixty-five population face similar challenges, but white men apparently have less experience coping with disappointments and setbacks, have further to fall in their status, and have fewer familial resources in comparison to other groups. For more information on suicide among those sixty-five and older, please see chapter 4, "Suicide and the Elderly."

○ *Is it true that more men than women commit suicide?*

Yes. Of the approximate thirty thousand people a year who take their lives, twenty-four thousand are men and six thousand are women.

○ *Why so many more men than women?*

This is one of those questions for which there's a lot of opinion and conjecture, but no clear answers. While far fewer women than men kill themselves, three times as many women as men *try* to kill themselves. Is this because more women than men want to die? Or is it because women are more likely to express their suicidal feelings than men but aren't usually as determined as men to actually kill themselves? Or is it that women are simply not as effective in killing themselves as men? Generally, women choose less lethal methods, like pills. But do they choose less lethal methods because they don't really want to die, or because they're less violent than men, or because they're more concerned with disfigurement, or because they have less access than men to guns?

These aren't the only possible explanations, but they are among those most commonly stated.

○ *What are the differences in suicide rates in terms of age?*

People between the ages of seventy-five and eighty-four have
the highest rate of suicide (22.8 per 100,000). People who are
eighty-five and older come in a close second (at a rate of 21.9
per 100,000).

Following is a list of rates per 100,000 by age group, in ten-
year increments. The numbers are from a report issued by the
U.S. Bureau of Vital Statistics for 1992.

AGE	RATES PER 100,000
5 to 14	0.9
15 to 24	13.0
25 to 34	14.5
35 to 44	15.1
45 to 54	14.7
55 to 64	14.8
65 to 74	16.5
75 to 84	22.8
85 and over	21.9

○ *Why do elderly people kill themselves in such large numbers?*

Elderly people often face greater challenges than do younger
people, from financial difficulties and ill health to loss of status
and the death of a longtime spouse. Please see chapter 4, "Suicide and the Elderly," for more information on this subject.

○ *What are the differences in suicide rates in terms of race?*

In this country, Native Americans have the highest rate of suicide, followed by white people, Japanese Americans, Chinese

Americans, Hispanics, African Americans, and Filipino Americans.

○ *Why the differences between the races and ethnic groups?*

There are no simple answers to this question, particularly because the differences and the reasons for them have not been thoroughly studied. But we do know that cultural and social as well as economic factors affect each group of people. And these factors affect men and women as well as the young and old in different ways.

For example, the suicide rate for black men is about half what it is for white men (12 per 100,000 versus 22 per 100,000). And among white men, the rate of suicide climbs dramatically in later life, reaching a peak in old age. For black men, the rate peaks in young adulthood, declines dramatically through midlife, and then begins to rise gradually after about age sixty.

There are a number of theories regarding the overall difference in suicide rates between black and white men as well as the differences at the various stages throughout life. (Please bear in mind that what I'm about to say involves some very broad generalizations.) One theory is that black men face far greater stresses early in life than do white men because of discrimination, poverty, and family disintegration. Having been tempered in early adulthood by these experiences, they are therefore better equipped to deal with the inevitable challenges and disappointments of life. White men, on the other hand—who do not have to deal with discrimination, are less likely to be poor, and are more likely to come from intact families—generally have higher expectations and less experience with disappointment. Lacking the coping skills black men acquire early in life, white men are more likely to be inexperienced in facing frustration and hopelessness, which leaves them more vulnerable to suicide, particularly as they age and lose status.

○ *Are people who have had a suicide in their family more likely to commit suicide? Does suicide run in families?*

Recently, I read in the newspaper a letter written to a national columnist by a woman who had lost several family members to suicide. On Christmas Day 1952 her sister committed suicide at age thirty-three. On April 8, 1992, her son committed suicide at age thirty-three. Two days later, her son's thirty-two-year-old wife committed suicide. And two months later, her son's mother-in-law committed suicide. Certainly, in this family, it appears that there is a more than coincidental pattern.

Another example is the family of writer Ernest Hemingway, whose father committed suicide in 1928 with a Civil War–era pistol. Ernest killed himself in 1962 by gunshot. His younger brother shot and killed himself in 1982. And one of his sisters also committed suicide.

As the son of a man who committed suicide, I have been concerned about this question ever since I first learned that those who have had a parent commit suicide are at greater risk of committing suicide themselves. That said, there is no clear agreement as to why family members are at greater risk of suicide. Grief and the depression that may follow a suicide (or any death, for that matter) are certainly contributing factors. Genetics may be involved as well, since depression and schizophrenia, which are leading factors associated with suicide, can be passed on through genetic material. Also, personality traits may be inherited that make a person more or less able to cope with life's challenges, and perhaps even self-destructive tendencies are inherited. Then there's the example set by someone who commits suicide, introducing into a family the idea of suicide as a realistic option for dealing with life.

For a more information on this subject, see chapter 7, "Coping with the Suicide of Someone You Know."

○ *Is it true that people who have AIDS commit suicide more frequently than people who have other illnesses? Why?*

For almost everyone I've known who has had AIDS, the suicide option is one that's been thoroughly discussed. And as Gina Kolata reported in the *New York Times* on June 14, 1994, according to several studies in New York, California, and Texas, people with AIDS kill themselves at a much higher rate than do people with other diseases, and the suicide rate among people with AIDS is from ten to twenty times that of the general population. Although there are no statistics on assisted suicide and AIDS, it's not much of a leap to figure that people with AIDS ask for help in dying at a greater rate as well.

There are several reasons for this high rate of suicide, including the nature of AIDS and the population affected. It's no secret how awful the end stages of the disease can be. In the relatively close-knit gay communities where AIDS has thus far had its greatest impact, people have had the opportunity to watch others go through the experience of dying, and suicide is generally widely discussed and seen as a rational and reasonable option for those in the very late stages of the illness.

There are other reasons as well for the high rate of suicide among AIDS patients. As the *New York Times* article points out, those suffering from AIDS also experience a range of stresses that leave people vulnerable to suicide, from financial

insecurity and homelessness to joblessness and social isolation. Other contributing factors include the depression and
delirium that can result from the disease itself or from any
number of the medications prescribed to combat the various
illnesses that affect AIDS patients.

○ *Are there certain professions in which people are more likely
to commit suicide?*

Yes. For example, police officers are more likely to commit
suicide than schoolteachers, doctors more likely than writers,
and writers more likely than the average person.

○ *What's with doctors? Don't they have it all?*

Well, they apparently have it all and more when it comes to
the stress their jobs place on their lives. What they apparently
don't have a lot of are the coping skills they need to deal with
that stress. Stress, combined with higher rates of alcohol abuse
than average, plus a reluctance to seek help, plus easy access
to potentially deadly drugs, translates into a suicide rate three
times that of the general population.

○ *Why are police officers more likely to kill themselves?*

Police officers have unusually stressful jobs, especially big-
city police officers, who unfortunately witness more than their
share of life's tragedies. And in general, these are not the kinds
of things they feel they can discuss with their loved ones. Also,
police officers who are having problems with their work
and/or their marriages are unlikely to seek professional help.

Part of the reason is the macho police culture, but not incidentally, officers who seek professional counseling may also fear jeopardizing their careers. Depending on a particular police department's regulations, officers who seek counseling may have to surrender their guns and/or be placed on restricted duty. And finally, perhaps most significantly, police officers have guns, and they know how to use them. Nine out of ten officers who commit suicide do so using their own guns.

○ *Why do writers have such a high suicide rate?*

As a writer, especially one who tends toward the occasional bleak mood, I find that this question makes me a little nervous. But the fact is that writers—as well as others in creative/artistic professions—are far more likely to have problems with depression than the average person, and that puts them at much greater risk of suicide. (We won't even talk about the isolation that goes along with being a writer and how that contributes to bleak thoughts.)

Kay Jamison, a professor of psychiatry at Johns Hopkins University and the author of *Touched with Fire: Manic-Depressive Illness and the Artistic Temperament*, was quoted in a November 14, 1994, article in the *New York Times* by William Grimes as saying that writers were ten to twenty times as likely as the general population to suffer manic-depressive or depressive illnesses, which lead to suicide more often than do any other mental disorders. Yikes! She goes on to say that "the cognitive style of manic-depression overlaps with the creative temperament. . . . When we think of creative writers, we think of boldness, sensitivity, restlessness, discontent; this is the manic-depressive temperament."

○ *Who are some well-known writers who have killed themselves?*

Sylvia Plath, Virginia Woolf, Ernest Hemingway, poet Anne Sexton, and Japanese novelist Yukio Mishima are but five on a painfully long list of writers and other creative artists who have taken their own lives. Then, of course, there are those who took the route of slow suicide and simply drank themselves to death.

○ *During which time of year are people most likely to commit suicide?*

Contrary to expectations, winter is not the time of year when people are most likely to kill themselves. According to A. Alvarez, as he writes in his book *The Savage God: A Study of Suicide,* "The cycle of self-destruction follows precisely that of nature: it declines in autumn, reaches its low in midwinter and then begins to rise slowly with the sap; its climax is in early summer, May and June; in July it gradually begins once more to drop." Alvarez goes on to suggest that it's the growing contrast between a suicidal depression and nature's annual rebirth that makes life increasingly intolerable. "The richer, softer and more delectable nature becomes, the deeper that internal abyss which separates the inner world from the outer. Thus suicide becomes a natural reaction to an unnatural condition."

An interesting footnote: in Belgium, as reported in the September 18, 1993, issue of *Science News,* a study of suicide found that violent suicide increases in April and May in adults younger than sixty-five and in August for people older than sixty-five.

○ *On which days of the week are people most likely to commit suicide?*

People are most likely to commit suicide on Friday or Monday. Apparently this is when people feel the loneliest.

○ *Where are people most likely to commit suicide?*

We're most likely to hear about a suicide when it's a very public event—for example, when someone jumps from a bridge. But most people take their lives in their homes or in close proximity to home.

○ *Is the rate of suicide the same in every state?*

No. The national average is about 12 suicides per 100,000. New Jersey has the lowest rate, at about 6.5 per 100,000. And Nevada has the highest, at about 25 per 100,000. Although California's rate of approximately 12 per 100,000 represents the national average, the western states in general have traditionally had higher rates of suicide.

○ *Why are suicide rates generally higher in the western states than in the eastern states?*

No one has come up with a definitive answer to this question, but a couple of contributing factors have been suggested that ring true. First, there's the traditional western frontier spirit of not needing help and the looser community and family ties of people who have moved west to get a fresh start. Then there's the problem with the very notion of getting a fresh start. People are often disappointed to discover that no matter where they go to get a fresh start, a lot of their old problems go with them. In an unfamiliar place, they're even less likely to have the support they need to deal with them.

○ *Which city in the United States has the highest rate of suicide?*

According to an article in the May 17, 1995, issue of the *San Francisco Bay Guardian*, San Francisco, perhaps the most beautiful city in the United States, has the highest rate of suicide of the twenty-five most populated cities in the country. According to the latest figures from the Centers for Disease Control (1992–93), San Francisco's rate of suicide was 16.8 per 100,000. Phoenix came in second, with a rate of 14.7. Los Angeles and New York City trailed, with rates below the national average: 10.8 and 10.4, respectively. And as Alan Saracevic reports in the *Guardian* article, "San Francisco's total represents an increase of more than 20 percent since 1989."

○ *Why San Francisco?*

In the *Bay Guardian* article just mentioned, Alan Saracevic lays out the various theories proposed by:
  1. Boyd Stevens, San Francisco's medical examiner:

  San Francisco has always been the city at the end of the rainbow. People come here with high ideals, and sometimes [things] just [don't] happen for them.

  2. Various psychiatrists, suicidologists, and doctors:

  The natural beauty and cultural advantages of San Francisco can be deceiving.

[The high rate is due to the] relatively high rates found in the general gay and lesbian populations and especially among people with HIV and AIDS.

The city's small geographic size causes tensions that encourage suicides.

3. Richard Seiden, a suicidologist, and Jerome Motto, a professor emeritus of psychiatry at the University of California at San Francisco: both Seiden and Motto believe that the city's relatively small geographic size gives the appearance of an alarming suicide rate. According to Seiden, "If you were to superimpose San Francisco onto Los Angeles, it shows that it would make much more sense to take a rate for the entire Bay Area, not just San Francisco. Manhattan is to New York what San Francisco is to the Bay Area. The numbers are diluted when you take into account the bedroom communities."

In the end, there's probably no single answer, and plenty of room for debate for years to come.

○ **What about the rates of suicide in other countries? Is it true that people are more likely to commit suicide in places like Sweden?**

Having spent a semester of college at the University of Copenhagen, from January to June of 1979, I've joked on more than one occasion that I know why Scandinavia has the highest suicide rates in the world. Between the incredibly short days of winter and the oppressive, gloomy weather, it made perfect sense to me, knowing very little about suicide at the time, that people would kill themselves in great numbers. The suicide rates in the Nordic countries are indeed high (29.2 in Finland, 21.4 in Denmark, 18 in Sweden, and 15.5 in Norway, according to World Health Organization statistics), but not as high as they are in Hungary, where the number is close to 40 per 100,000.

At the other end of the statistics scale are Italy, at 7.2, Brazil at 5.3, and Jamaica at 0.4 per 100,000.

Just for the sake of comparison, the rate in Great Britain is 7.8 and in Japan is 15.8 per 100,000.

○ *Have people always committed suicide?*

The first recorded reference to suicide appears in *The Dispute Between a Man and His Ba,* which was written four thousand years ago "in the first intermediate period of the Middle Kingdom in Egypt." It was written by "a man who is tired of life and buffeted by ill fortune [and] considers killing himself." (Colt, p. 130)

Throughout recorded history—and for a variety of reasons, from the need to preserve one's honor and the desire to sacrifice oneself for the greater good to depression and terminal illness—people have committed suicide, from Socrates, Brutus, and Nero to Van Gogh, Jackson Pollock, and Kurt Cobain. It's reasonable to assume that people committed suicide prior to recorded history as well.

○ *How have attitudes toward suicide changed over the centuries?*

Today in Western society, as George Howe Colt notes in *The Enigma of Suicide,* we generally consider suicide a psychiatric problem. "We study it, search for its causes, and struggle to prevent what we consider a tragic and sometimes shameful act." But that's not how it always was, which makes this a re-

markably complex question to answer. Over the centuries, different cultures have had different attitudes toward suicide depending on their spiritual beliefs and attitudes toward death in
general, and those attitudes have changed over time.

For example, A. Alvarez writes in his book *The Savage God*
that among the Vikings, only those who died a violent death
could enter paradise, or Valhalla. "The greatest honor and the
greatest qualification was death in battle; next best was suicide.
Those who died peacefully in their beds, of old age or disease,
were excluded from Valhalla through all eternity." Among the
ancient Scythians, it was considered "the greatest honor to
take their own lives when they became too old for their no-
madic way of life; thereby saving the younger members of the
tribe both the trouble and the guilt of killing them."

For the ancient Greeks, Alvarez notes, the act of suicide
"passes more or less without comment, certainly without
blame. . . . So far as the records go, the ancient Greeks took
their lives only for the best possible reasons: grief, high patri-
otic principle, or to avoid dishonor." And whereas the Greeks
tolerated suicide, the Romans, according to George Howe
Colt, "made it a fashion, even a sport."

Early Christian teachings, according to Alvarez, were "at
first a powerful incitement to suicide." He notes, "The more
powerfully the Church instilled in believers the idea that this
world was a vale of tears and sin and temptation, where they
waited uneasily until death released them into eternal glory,
the more irresistible the temptation to suicide became. . . .
Why, then, live unredeemed when heavenly bliss is only a
knife stroke away?" It wasn't until the sixth century A.D., following countless suicides committed in the name of eternal
glory, that Christian attitudes shifted and funeral rites were

"refused to all suicides regardless of social position, reason or method."

In Japan today, the attitude toward suicide as well as the methods and reasons people commit suicide generally mirror what prevails in the West. But historically, according to George Howe Colt, "suicide in Japan has enjoyed not only religious tolerance but state approval. The romantic aura that surrounds suicide grew out of the development of *seppuku*, a traditional form of suicide better known outside Japan as *harakiri*, or 'belly-cutting.' It was practiced by the samurai, or military class, who followed an ethical code known as *Bushido* — 'the way of the knights.'" Colt notes that "*seppuku* originated about a thousand years ago during the beginning of Japanese feudalism as an honorable way for a soldier to avoid the humiliation of capture."

Here are just a few more examples of different attitudes across cultures, as noted by Colt: "The Bannaus of Cambodia buried suicides in a corner of the forest; natives of Dahomey left the bodies of suicides in the fields to be devoured by wild beasts. The Alabama Indians threw them into the river. Among the Wajagga of East Africa, after a man hanged himself a goat was sacrificed with the same noose in hopes of mollifying the dead man's soul."

For in-depth discussions of the history of suicide and differing attitudes across cultures, I recommend both A. Alvarez's *The Savage God* and George Howe Colt's *The Enigma of Suicide*, both of which are listed in the appendix.

○ *How was suicide dealt with in America in past centuries?*

Before the twentieth century, suicide was generally viewed as both a crime and a sin. Three centuries ago, for example, in colonial America, if you committed suicide, you could not count on a standard church burial. In Massachusetts, for example, the "Self-Murther" act, which was passed in 1660, stipulated, "If any person Inhabitant or Stranger, shall at any time be found by any Jury to lay violent hands on themselves, or be wilfully guilty of their own Death, every person shall be denied the privilege of being Buried in the Common Burying place of Christians, but shall be Buried in some Common High-way where the Select-men of the Town where such person did inhabit shall appoint, and a Cart-load of Stones laid upon the Grave as a Brand of Infamy, and as a warning to others to beware of the like Damnable practices."

In England during that same period, the deceased was tried posthumously in the coroner's court. If found guilty, as George Howe Colt explains in *The Enigma of Suicide*, the usual penalty was "property confiscation and burial at a crossroads with a wooden stake through the heart." The only way to avoid this fate was for a jury to rule that the deceased had acted from insanity. The last recorded burial at a crossroads as punishment for suicide took place in 1823.

Colt notes that the colonies were more lenient. For example, he cites William Penn's charter to Pennsylvania in 1700, in which he recommended "that if any person, through temptation or melancholy, shall destroy himself, his estate, real and personal, shall, notwithstanding, descend to his wife, children, or relations, as if he had died a natural death."

○ *Why do people commit or try to commit suicide?*

For those of us who have lived through the suicide of a loved one, this is the question that is just about guaranteed to haunt us for the rest of our lives. And even if we know some of the specific reasons a loved one has taken his or her life, we're still left wondering why. Why did the person do it? Was it hopelessness? Was it the emotional pain of depression? What could it have been? And why didn't the person ask for help?

In answering this question, I'll talk about many of the reasons people kill themselves, from the personal to the political. But if you're looking for an answer that will satisfy your desire to know why your loved one chose to commit suicide, I'm afraid you'll probably be disappointed, because for most people, there is no satisfying answer.

As you read through the reasons that follow, keep in mind that although a reason may be listed here, its presence in someone's life is not necessarily sufficient reason for that person to commit suicide. For example, many people experience sudden loss, such as the death of a spouse, but don't commit suicide; yet for other people, who may already be struggling with depression, the death of a spouse could be the event that pushes them over the edge.

PSYCHOLOGICAL/PHYSIOLOGICAL REASONS
Depression

I'm not talking here about the everyday kind of depression we all have experienced. This is major, incapacitating depression—what the writer William Styron in *Darkness Visible*, his remarkable book about his own suicidal depression, calls "the despair beyond the despair." It's the kind of depression that is so painful it leads some people to take their lives. Styron writes, "The pain of severe depression is quite unimaginable to those who have not suffered it, and it kills in many instances because its anguish can no longer be borne." For more on this subject, see the discussion of the question on depression later in this chapter. I also highly recommend Styron's eloquent and insightful book, in which he describes his descent into and recovery from a suicidal depression; it is listed in the appendix.

Schizophrenia, Personality Disorder, etc.

People who suffer from a variety of mental disorders have a higher risk of suicide.

Alcoholism and Substance Abuse

People who abuse alcohol and other drugs are at higher risk of suicide. Besides the personal and professional stresses they bring on, alcohol and substance abuse also impair judgment and allow people to act on self-destructive feelings they might not otherwise respond to in such a drastic way.

Illness and Physical Infirmity

Physical pain, infirmity brought on by old age or illness, and terminal disease all lead some people to take their lives. Some of these people commit suicide because their pain is unbearable. Others are afraid of not being able to care for themselves, and still others are concerned about placing a financial, physical, and emotional burden on their families.

   Some people who are terminally ill ask for and receive assistance in taking their lives. For more information on this topic, see chapter 8, "Assisted Suicide."

Revenge, Anger, Punishment

After thirty years of marriage, Leslie finally got up the courage to ask her husband for a separation. "The fact is I knew in the first months of the marriage that this was a mistake, but it took me a little while—and putting three kids through college—to finally make the move. I was always afraid my husband would do something crazy if we divorced, so I only asked for a separation." Leslie's husband moved out, and over the next several months they remained in contact and continued talking, although Leslie was firm about not wanting to get back together. "It was our thirty-first wedding anniversary, and I was feeling a little down. I came home from work, walked in the front door, and there he was sprawled on the entryway floor. There was blood everywhere. Do you think he was trying to tell me something? I try not to blame myself, because I know that's what he wanted."

Leslie's husband used his suicide to send a very definite and angry message. Other people use suicide or the threat of suicide in the same way: "If you won't do *x*, I'm going to kill myself." Or the thinking, particularly among young people, may go: "I'll kill myself and then you'll really be sorry." Ironically, if these people kill themselves, they won't be around to witness the punishment they've inflicted on their loved ones.

FOR THE COMMUNITY, FOR THE GREATER GOOD, FOR A CAUSE
Sacrifice for Others or the Community

A year ago I heard a story on the news about an elderly couple in Florida. She had Alzheimer's disease. He had severe asthma. Money wasn't a problem. They had $10 million in the bank. In their note to their family, they explained that they knew they had enough money to be cared for but preferred that the money be spent on young people who could make things better for everyone. The couple went into their garage, got in the car, turned on the ignition, and died. The pastor at their church said they took "the high road to death."

This story reminds me of traditional Eskimo culture, where in lean times the sick and/or elderly went off on their own to die in order to conserve the community's limited resources and to ensure the community's survival. A more contemporary example is that of an unemployed parent who commits suicide knowing that the insurance money will assure the family of the financial support he or she cannot provide.

Another example, which we may not think of as suicide, is that of a soldier who sacrifices his life in order to save his buddies, or a mother who throws a child out of harm's way knowing that she'll be sacrificing her own life in the process.

One more example is the story of a young man who killed himself at age twenty-seven. His mother wrote a letter to the editor of the *New York Times* in response to an article entitled "Quest for Evolutionary Meaning in the Persistence of Suicide." She wrote: "Peter, who was brilliant, left us a 60-minute tape, honestly describing his condition of pain, which began when he was 17. In the next 10 years he managed to do a tour in the Army, finish college, teach math in a Roman Catholic school in Guam and write three books for major publishers — while continually fighting the lure of death. He described his own condition for us, strikingly telling us he had 'a missing part,' he was 'a Rolls-Royce — but without spark plugs.' Yet underlying all of this in the last year of his life was his paralyzing fear that he would become violent. I have often wondered if my incredibly sensitive son killed himself to make sure this never happened."

Politics

Suicide is used on rare occasion to make a political statement, as it was by two men in their twenties in Korea in 1987. Both men were apparently distraught over the failure of opposition leaders to unite behind a single presidential candidate and intended their acts of self-immolation as a protest.

Suicide bombers also use suicide to achieve political goals. For more on that subject, please read on.

Suicide Bombers

These are people who sacrifice their lives in order to accomplish an assassination or widespread destruction of life and property for a political and/or military goal. Often they are motivated by the belief that in committing this act they will achieve honor and, depending on their religious beliefs, gain quick entry into heaven.

During the waning days of World War II, decades before they became relatively commonplace in the Middle East as a part of war and political struggle, suicide bombers played a role in the Pacific. Japanese kamikaze pilots, who were named after the "divine wind" that destroyed Genghis Khan's ships as they sailed toward Japan, crashed their planes into enemy ships, sacrificing their lives in order to disable or destroy their targets. As reported by the Associated Press in 1994, these attacks resulted in the sinking of thirty-four American ships and the deaths of 4,907 sailors—"a fifth of the Navy's casualties in World War II."

Social Custom

For hundreds of years in India, it was customary—George Howe Colt refers to it as a blend of choice and coercion—for a woman "to throw herself on her husband's funeral pyre to prove her devotion." The practice is called *suttee*, and although it was outlawed by the British in 1829, it occurs on occasion to this day. (Colt, pp. 136–37)

SUDDEN LOSS, TRAUMA, OUTSIDE THREAT

Loss of a Loved One

Whether it's the sudden death of a loved one or a best friend, or the breakup—or threatened breakup—of a marriage or relationship, some people are driven by loss to take their own lives.

In 1993, when football player Jeff Alm, a Houston Oiler, accidentally crashed his car into a freeway guard rail, killing his best friend, he shot and killed himself only moments later. As reported by the Associated Press, "Alm, apparently distraught, . . . took a shotgun from the trunk of his car and shot himself in the face."

Another example is that of a young woman in Queens, New York, who jumped from the sixteenth floor of her family's apartment house two days after her fiancé was murdered by a man who had been obsessed with her. Apparently it was the shock and grief over her loss that led to the suicide.

Loss of Job, Economic Distress

During hard economic times, when companies lay off employees or farms are threatened with foreclosure, some people, consumed by depression and a sense of hopelessness, see no way out of their predicament other than suicide.

Sexual Orientation, Gender Conflicts

It might seem a bit odd to place the topic of sexual orientation and gender conflicts (for example, men who want to be women and women who want to be men) in this section, but many of the problems experienced by gay, lesbian, bisexual, and transgender people have to do with the pressures and prejudices of society. These added pressures and prejudices can result in psychological conflicts and depression as well as alcoholism and drug abuse—all of which put members of these groups, especially adolescents, at greater risk of suicide.

Public Humiliation, Scandal

On more than one occasion we've seen the headlines: So-and-So Public Official About to be Indicted Commits Suicide. One of those times the public official was someone I used to work for—the borough president of Queens, New York. I'd been his speechwriter briefly in 1984. Shortly after he was implicated in a bribery scandal, he attempted suicide and wound up in the hospital. I remember seeing all the negative press coverage after his release and thinking, *He's going to try again.* I could just imagine the screaming headlines intensifying his depression and making him feel even more humiliated and trapped by his situation. And, in fact, he did try again, this time putting a knife through his heart and dying on the floor of his kitchen.

Of course, it's not only public officials caught in scandals or in humiliating circumstances who feel trapped by their circumstances and see suicide as the only way out. They're just the ones we're more likely to hear about.

Outside Threat

All kinds of outside threats—including genocide, war, blackmail, and extortion—have driven individuals as well as groups of people to commit suicide.

Eve R. Meyer, the executive director of San Francisco Suicide Prevention, told me the story of her parents' escape from a concentration camp during World War II. When they were prevented by a guard from crossing the border from France into Spain in their attempt to flee the Nazis, they decided they would kill themselves rather than risk being caught and returned to the camps and certain death. Ms. Meyer said, "I didn't learn this story until I was an adult. My brother told me how my father took my mother's hand and the two of them turned to my brother and grandmother and took their hands and said, 'We're not going back. We're going to walk into the ocean.' My brother, who was eight or nine, fought them, but they dragged him across the beach to the water's edge. The guard caught up with them and told them it was a mistake and said they could go through. My parents never talked about it."

Nearly two thousand years earlier, 967 Jews killed themselves at Massada, in what is now Israel, rather than submit to the Roman forces that had encircled their mountaintop fortress.

The most poignant contemporary story I came across in which an outside threat contributed to a suicide was that of Kiyoteru Okouchi, a thirteen-year-old Japanese boy who committed suicide by hanging himself from a tree in the family garden on November 27, 1994. Andrew Pollack of the *New York Times* wrote a compelling account of what led Kiyoteru to take his life. As Pollack reported, "For more than a year, four of his classmates had been demanding money from him, sometimes hundreds of dollars at a time. Once, when he would not comply, they held his head under water in a river. Another time they forced him to undress and left him in the gymnasium in his underwear." The young boy left behind a suicide note and a diary in which he gave a detailed account of the extortion and named his tormentors. Included along with the suicide note and his diary was a note to his mother promising to pay her back "the roughly $11,000 he had taken to give the bullies."

○ *Do suicide notes offer any clues as to why people kill themselves?*

It turns out that only about one in five or six people who kill themselves leaves a note behind. And even those who leave notes don't necessarily reveal anything that would be helpful in understanding what led them to kill themselves. As George Howe Colt writes in *The Enigma of Suicide*, "For many years researchers believed that notes held a key to understanding motivation for suicide, but several dozen studies have revealed little more than that suicide notes reflect the range of emotions of suicidal people."

That said, there are suicide notes that provide valuable insight regarding the motives or the circumstances that led to a suicide. For example, the thirteen-year-old Japanese boy I wrote about above left a note in which he explained how he had been subject to the bullying and extortion of his classmates. In his note he said: "They took money from me, including 1,000 yen my grandmother had given me and the money I planned to use for having my hair cut. I had to cut my own hair. I should have committed suicide earlier but did not for the sake of my family."

Included in an exhibition of suicide notes at a New York City gallery was one that also offered tragic insight into a child's suicide. As reported in the *New York Times*, the note said, "Dear Dad, Don't fell sory or sad. I lied and lied. I got an f in english because it was a 10th grade class. I carry on in school up in [heaven] I wonder if they have a football teem up in [heaven] and I'll go look for Grampa and Granny. Happy Easter." The boy who wrote the note was only twelve, and he shot himself.

I didn't learn that my father had left a suicide note until my mother handed me a photocopy of it ten years after he died.

She found it tucked in a drawer and thought I'd be interested in seeing it. I was, although I was disappointed that there was no mention in the note of me or my sister and brother. In the handwritten note he talked about being in a lot of pain and how we'd be better off without him. This was not an easy letter to read, although the rest of it was about practical matters, such as legal documents and his savings account. The whole thing was remarkably dispassionate, especially given the monumentality of the moment. I don't know how I could possibly have done so, but I promptly lost the copy of the note and have never been able to find it. There are no other known copies, and the original was apparently misplaced shortly after my father's suicide.

Not everyone who leaves a message behind leaves it in the form of a note. Some people leave tapes, as did the comedienne Joan Rivers's husband, Edgar Rosenberg, when he committed suicide in 1987. According to an account in *People* magazine, he left two manila envelopes, one for Joan and one for his daughter, Melissa, in the Philadelphia hotel room where he took an overdose of Valium mixed with alcohol. "Each [envelope] was marked with three kisses—XXX. They found that in his meticulous way, Edgar was putting their affairs in order, sending them papers for estate planning, lists of the contents of the house, bank account numbers, his case of keys. . . . On tape cassettes were his personal messages."

○ *Why do young children attempt or commit suicide?*

More than three hundred children a year, aged five to fourteen (three quarters of them male), take their own lives. Hundreds, perhaps thousands, more try, and with each passing year, as they choose increasingly lethal methods, more are succeeding. Many of the children who attempt or commit suicide suffer from depression, often as a result of having been abused or neglected. Some try to kill themselves to join a loved one who has died. Others, like the Japanese boy mentioned earlier, are bullied or teased by their peers and see no other way out.

The Olympic diving champion Greg Louganis attempted suicide for the first time when he was twelve years old. Since early childhood Louganis had suffered from depression. At the time of the attempt he was feeling alienated from his adoptive parents and his classmates at school. What pushed him over the edge was the news from his doctor that he'd have to quit gymnastics because his already damaged knees couldn't take the continued pounding of his daily workouts. He said, "I'd hoped to compete in gymnastics at the Olympics one day, but now that dream was gone. . . . I went into my parents' medicine cabinet and took a bunch of different pills, mostly aspirin and Ex-Lax. Then I took a razor blade out of the cabinet and started playing with it over my wrist. I started to bleed, but I didn't go deep enough to cut any veins or arteries. It also turned out that I didn't take enough of anything from the medicine cabinet to cause myself harm. . . . Afterward, I was even more angry and depressed, because I didn't see any way out."

Louganis's depression went undiagnosed for years and contributed to two more suicide attempts in his teens and early twenties.

○ *What role does depression play in suicide?*

Depression plays a tremendous role, but not just run-of-the-mill depression. Everyone has experienced plain old "normal" depression. It's awful. You feel melancholy. You lack energy. It's like having a bad cold, and, like a cold, it passes relatively quickly.

The kind of depression I'm talking about here is "major" depression or clinical depression, the kind that doesn't go away so quickly, lasting two or more weeks. According to the National Institute of Mental Health, fifteen percent of the people who suffer from this form of depression ultimately commit suicide.

Symptoms of major depression include a depressed or irritable mood, a loss of interest or pleasure in usual activities, changes in appetite and weight, disturbed sleep, motor retardation or agitation, fatigue and loss of energy, feelings of worthlessness, self-reproach, excessive guilt, difficulty in thinking or concentrating, and suicidal thinking or suicide attempts.

If you're experiencing this kind of depression or someone you love is in the midst of a major depression, do not ignore it. It is serious, and it requires more than kind words and warm milk. You need to find a mental-health professional who has experience in treating people suffering from major depression. Call your doctor or local community mental-health center to get a referral. Or call one of the local crisis centers listed in the appendix of this book. Major depression can be treated, so make that call and get help for yourself or someone you care about.

○ *Is it true that people whose suicidal feelings result from clinical depression are at greater risk of suicide once they start treatment?*

This may sound crazy, but it's true. People who are severely depressed and suicidal may be so impaired by their depression that they don't have the energy or wherewithal to follow through on a desire to commit suicide. Once treatment begins and the patient starts coming back to life—but before the depression and suicidal feelings are gone—there's the danger that the person will now have enough energy to act on his or her suicidal feelings. Mental-health professionals who treat major depression know this and closely monitor their patients. This is one reason it's so important to seek the help of a mental-health professional who is experienced in treating major depression. It's not enough to see your family physician for a prescription for antidepressants. Major depression isn't bronchitis, and there's no magic pill that will cure it.

○ *Is schizophrenia a cause of suicide?*

Schizophrenia, which is a type of mental illness, does not cause suicide, but approximately 10 percent of those who suffer from it eventually commit suicide.

○ *What role does alcohol play in suicide?*

Alcohol plays an enormous role in suicide. As the psychologist Paul G. Quinnett points out in his book *Suicide: The Forever Decision*, alcohol removes fear and exaggerates moods—good and bad. Under the influence of alcohol we're likely to think and do things we wouldn't when sober. That's one of the appealing aspects of alcohol: it can take us out of ourselves and give us the freedom to think, do, and say things we wouldn't when sober. Unfortunately, when it comes to acting on bad feelings, including suicidal impulses, alcohol is a particularly deadly lubricant. Studies have shown that around 90 percent of alcoholics and more than a third of nonalcoholics who commit suicide had been drinking prior to taking their lives. And then, of course, there are those people who use alcohol to commit a form of slow suicide by drinking themselves to death.

Jeff Alm, the Houston Oiler whose death I mentioned in discussing an earlier question, accidentally crashed his car on a Houston freeway, causing his best friend to be thrown to his death. Alm then took a shotgun from his car and killed himself. When I first heard the story I was sure alcohol was involved, and I soon learned that it was. A few weeks after the crash, medical officials reported that at his death Alm had had a blood-alcohol level of 0.14 percent (the legal driving limit is 0.10). One can imagine that Alm's despair and guilt were intensified by the alcohol in his blood, that the alcohol reduced his fear and impaired his thinking as he took the gun from his car, placed it against his head, and pulled the trigger. Both Alm and his friend were twenty-five years old.

○ *What role does hopelessness play in suicide?*

Almost all of us have experienced a sense of hopelessness at one time or another that things wouldn't get better, that we didn't have any options. And most of us who experience hopelessness get over it. But others don't, and these people are in significant danger of doing themselves harm.

In *Suicide: The Forever Decision*, Paul Quinnett says that hopelessness "is the one common thread among the majority of those who elect the suicide option. Despairing of any future or solution to their problems, the utterly hopeless frequently find themselves thinking, 'What's the use? I might as well be dead.'"

If you're feeling hopeless, if you feel trapped, if you are indeed thinking that you might as well be dead, you need help in getting over these feelings. As I suggested in the discussion of the question about depression, find a mental-health professional. There are always options in life—even when you think there are none. And the first option you have is getting help. Take it.

○ *What role do genetics and/or biology play in suicide?*

There is general agreement on the part of people who study suicide that genetics and/or biology play some role in suicide. How large a role and what exactly that role is, is open to much debate. The possibilities are intriguing, but nothing about this aspect of understanding suicide is set in stone. Following are a couple of the possibilities.

Suicidal behavior may or may not be inherited, but apparently major depression as well as other psychological disorders that increase the risk of suicide can be passed from generation to generation.

People who commit suicide are more likely to have a brain-chemical imbalance than those who don't. One brain chemical that has received special attention and is apparently related to suicide is a substance called *serotonin*, which is one of many neurotransmitters that control what brain cells do. Low levels of serotonin have been linked to depressed people who have committed suicide, but as George Howe Colt points out in *The Enigma of Suicide*, "it is not known whether the low levels are a cause or an effect of depression or impulsiveness." Clearly, this is an aspect of suicide that remains an enigma.

What makes the biological/genetic issue so compelling is the possibility that if clearly identifiable biological/genetic factors for suicidal behavior are found, corresponding treatments can be developed.

CHAPTER 2

HOW?

Before I say anything about how people kill themselves, I want to make it absolutely clear that this section is *not* a "how-to" for people contemplating suicide. I've chosen to write about how people take their lives to help you better understand suicide, not to give you or anyone else ideas.

If you are having strong suicidal feelings and are looking for the best way to do it, you've come to the wrong place. You need to get help, and I urge you to contact a local suicide-prevention hot line or one of the resources listed in the appendix.

○ *How do people commit suicide?*

In general, if it can cause harm it has been tried at least once, but most people commit suicide using one of a handful of methods. These include firearms, hanging, drugs, motor-vehicle exhaust, and jumping from high places.

Less frequently used methods include suffocation by plastic bag, drowning, slashing, natural gas, crashing cars, crashing airplanes, jumping from airplanes, electrocution, starvation, jumping from or in front of moving vehicles, injection of any number of agents, burns, cold, explosives, and leaping into an active volcano.

○ *Leaping into a volcano?*

This is by far the exception, given that most people don't live near volcanoes. But it happens. As George Howe Colt explains in *The Enigma of Suicide*, the only case in modern times of large numbers of people throwing themselves into an active volcano took place at Mihara-Yama, a volcano on the island of Oshima, about sixty miles from Tokyo. In 1933, Mieko Ueki, a twenty-four-year-old student, decided to throw herself into the volcano after becoming enchanted with a legend that said that those who committed suicide in this manner would be immediately cremated and sent to heaven in the form of smoke. Mieko's story itself quickly became a modern legend, inspiring many others to follow her lead. By the time authorities intervened and blocked access to the mountain in 1935, an estimated 800 men and 140 women had thrown themselves into the crater of the volcano.

○ *What is the method most often used to commit suicide?*

In the United States, more people use guns to kill themselves than any other means; guns account for approximately 60 percent of the thirty thousand annually reported suicides. And the popularity of firearms as a means of committing suicide is growing.

○ *Are the statistics different in countries that have strict gun-control laws?*

Yes, in Great Britain, for example, where private gun ownership is highly restricted, the use of guns in suicide ranks fifth.

○ *After guns, what are the most common means by which people commit suicide in the United States?*

The National Center for Health Statistics lumps together hanging, strangulation, and suffocation as the second most common way in which people kill themselves—methods that accounted for 4,484 deaths in 1989, or 15 percent of all suicides for that year. Of the people who used these methods to commit suicide, 4,084 used hanging, 303 used suffocation by plastic bag, and the rest strangled themselves in a variety of ways. (Because of the time-consuming nature of the way in which these statistics are compiled, 1989 was the most recent year for which complete figures on suicide *by method* were available.)

Following is a list in descending order of the primary methods—after guns, hanging, strangulation, and suffocation—used by people who committed suicide in the United States in 1989, along with the total number of cases of each:

○ Solid or liquid substances—3,215. Tranquilizers and other psychotropic agents accounted for 1,072 of the total cases. Arsenic accounted for only 9 of them.

○ Gases (other than domestic gas)—2,203. Motor-vehicle exhaust accounted for 1,814 of the total cases, although this number has been decreasing over the years due to emission control laws, which make this method of suicide less effective than in the past.

- Jumping from high places—712. Of this total, in 330 cases people jumped from residential buildings; in 282, from other manmade structures, including office buildings and bridges; in 20, from natural sites; 80 cases were unspecified.
- Cutting and piercing—418.
- Drowning—405.
- Jumping from or lying in front of moving objects (cars, trains, etc.)—236.
- Burns, fire—164.
- Crashing motor vehicles—64.
- Domestic gas (gas used in domestic situations—i.e., natural gas)—25.
- Electrocution—18.
- Crashing aircraft—1.

- *Crashing aircraft? Was this the guy who crashed his airplane into the White House?*

No, the above statistics are from 1989. The man who killed himself by crashing an airplane into the White House did so on Monday, September 12, 1994, at about 2 A.M. Frank Corder flew a stolen single-engine, two-seat airplane into the side of the White House, about thirty feet from President and Mrs. Clinton's bedroom. (The First Family was not at home at the time.) Corder, who was thirty-eight, had struggled with a drug and alcohol problem for a number of years and suffered from depression. Family members said he'd spoken of suicide before and, a year before his death, had said to his older brother, "If you're going to kill yourself, the way to do it is to take an airplane and crash it into the White House." In an interview with *People* magazine, his brother said, "Of course, everybody thought he was joking."

○ *Don't more than twenty-five people a year kill themselves by means of natural gas?*

There's no knowing how many people *attempt* suicide by putting their heads in gas ovens, but very few succeed, because natural gas used in homes is not nearly as lethal as people think.

○ *So where did people get the idea that putting their head in an oven and turning on the gas was an effective way to commit suicide?*

One strong possibility is that at one time, in England at least, putting one's head in an oven and turning on the gas was a very effective way to kill oneself. As George Howe Colt explains in *The Enigma of Suicide*, "For many years the most popular method of suicide in Great Britain was asphyxiation—sticking one's head in the oven and turning on the gas. After the discovery of oil and natural gas deposits in the North Sea in the fifties and sixties, most English homes converted from coke gas, whose high carbon monoxide content made it highly lethal, to less toxic natural gas. From 1963 to 1978 the number of English suicides by gas dropped from 2,368 to eleven."

○ *Are you sure the numbers are correct for suffocation with a plastic bag? I thought it was a common way people killed themselves, especially those who are terminally ill.*

The numbers I've listed are the *official* figures. You'll have a hard time finding anyone who believes that these are the true statistics on suicide. However, some numbers, like those for suicide from guns, are probably closer to the truth than others. It's a lot harder to disguise a self-inflicted gunshot to the head than it is to disguise death from suffocation.

Suffocation by plastic bag is indeed used in the suicides and assisted suicides of the terminally ill, but it's anyone's guess as to how often, because these deaths are only rarely reported as suicides. In these circumstances it's especially easy to disguise death by suffocation, for two reasons: death appears natural, and it's expected. And even if the doctor signing the death certificate knows that death wasn't from natural causes, he or she may look the other way and report it as a natural death. For more on assisted suicide, see chapter 8, "Assisted Suicide."

Whatever the real figures on suffocation with a plastic bag, it does appear that this method of suicide has grown more popular since the 1991 publication of *Final Exit,* a controversial suicide instruction book that recommends swallowing a quantity of sleeping pills before securing a plastic bag over one's head. In the seven years preceding the publication of the book, the average number of suicides by this method was 271. In 1991, the figure was 437. No direct link has yet been established between *Final Exit* and the increase, but I would venture a guess that the book was a significant contributing factor.

○ *How do you die from suffocation with a plastic bag?*

Death is caused by a lack of oxygen. As Sherwin B. Nuland writes in *How We Die: Reflections on Life's Final Chapter,* "Because the bag is so small, the oxygen is used up quickly. . . . Rapid cerebral failure ensues, but what really causes death is that a low blood-oxygen level slows the heart quickly to a complete standstill and the arrest of circulation. . . . Dr. Wayne Carver, the chief medical examiner of the state of Connecticut, has seen enough of such suicides to assure me that their faces are neither blue nor swollen. They look, in fact, quite ordinary—just dead."

○ *Can you tell me more about* Final Exit?

Final Exit, a suicide "how-to" book, was published in March 1991 and quickly became a best-seller. It was written by Derek Humphry, a cofounder of the Hemlock Society.

Humphry's book has drawn stern criticism from all corners of society for its explicit instructions on how to take one's life. Sherwin Nuland refers to *Final Exit* derisively as an "ill-advised cookbook of death." He focuses his criticism on the potential impact the book may have on the many young Americans who are known to try suicide each year, "plus an undiscoverable other huge group of those whose attempts are never disclosed."

Nuland quotes a June 1992 letter to the *Journal of the American Medical Association* from two psychiatrists at the Yale Child Study Center. They wrote: "With its lurid examples, explicit instructions, and vigorous advocacy for suicide, *Final Exit* may have an especially pernicious effect on adolescents, who, with their high rate of attempted and completed suicide, appear susceptible to imitative influences and cultural factors that glorify or destigmatize suicide."

○ *Why do people choose the methods they do?*

In general, the method people use to kill themselves depends on a number of things—from their sex, age, occupation, mental state or psychology, and degree of desperation, to the availability of a particular method, to custom and politics.

○ *How do methods differ by sex?*

When it comes to completed suicides, guns are the most frequently used method for both men and women, although men use firearms 65 percent of the time, and women 40 percent. At one time, the most frequently used method for women was drug overdose, but by the late 1980s guns had moved ahead of drugs as the method of choice.

○ *How do methods differ by age?*

The older people are, the more lethal the methods they choose. For example, elderly people are more likely to use guns to commit suicide than are people in their twenties.

Eve R. Meyer, the executive director of San Francisco Suicide Prevention, a private, nonprofit organization that runs the nation's oldest volunteer suicide hot-line service, explained that elderly people choose more lethal means because they've had "plenty of time to think about what they're doing. They're not impulsive. They have greater access to the means. And they're deadly serious." For more on the elderly and suicide, see chapter 4, "Suicide and the Elderly."

Young people, on the other hand, tend to be more impulsive and have less access to lethal means than do their elders. So they're unlikely to have carefully thought out what they're doing and more likely to use less lethal means to attempt suicide. The result is that they're not as likely to complete a suicide as are their elders. For more on young people and suicide, see chapter 3, "Teen/Youth Suicide."

○ *How do methods differ by occupation?*

Some occupations put the means of suicide within relatively
easy reach. For example, policemen have ready access to
firearms, and, not surprisingly, most policemen who kill themselves use guns. Among physicians, who are far more likely
than policemen to have access to drugs, 55 percent of those
who take their own lives use drugs, whereas dentists are more
likely to use anesthetic gas. (Colt, p. 235)

○ *How do methods differ by availability?*

Beyond differing availability based on occupation, which was
discussed in the answer to the previous question, there are
other factors that affect the availability of the means of self-
destruction. In cities with tall buildings, like Chicago and
Boston, or places that have spectacular ravines, such as the
campus of Cornell University, which has become somewhat
notorious for this reason, more people jump to their deaths
than in places with flat terrain and two-story buildings. Prisoners tend to hang themselves. And people who have easy access
to prescription medication are more likely to choose drugs to
end their lives than someone who does not. My father, for example, was taking a sedative prescribed by a doctor at the Veterans Administration hospital where he was being treated for
emotional problems. Over time he set aside pills, and when he
was ready he took enough to end his life.

○ *What impact does an individual's mental state—or psychological motivation—have on choice of method?*

Over the years, psychiatrists and psychologists have come up
with all sorts of deep—and sometimes bizarre—psychological

interpretations regarding the methods by which people choose to kill themselves. What seems more relevant is how the method sometimes expresses a person's feelings about herself or himself, or feelings for those left behind.

For example, someone who is very angry at himself may specifically choose a violent method of committing suicide. Or someone who is trying to punish, blame, or take revenge on those left behind may choose a method that sends a very obvious message. William, a young man of nineteen, climbed into the back of his family's station wagon one night, lay down, and shot himself in the head. He and his parents had been feuding for months over his choice of girlfriend, and he'd been forbidden to use the family car to drive to see her. William didn't leave a suicide note, but his message to his parents was clear.

Some people choose a method of suicide, such as a drug overdose, that will specifically spare their families the pain of discovering a disfigured body.

○ *How does method differ according to custom?*

Custom has less bearing today than it did in centuries past. But in various cultures throughout history, different methods of suicide were customary, almost fashionable. For example, in ancient Greece, death by hemlock was popular; in Rome, the fashionable way to commit suicide was to fall on your sword or open your veins in a warm bath. In nineteenth-century Paris, drowning yourself in the Seine became popular. In India widows were compelled to throw themselves on the funeral pyres of their husbands. And in Japan, samurais used knives to cut open their bellies. (Colt, pp. 233–35)

○ *What impact can politics possibly have on a chosen method of suicide?*

People kill themselves in a variety of ways, from starvation and self-immolation to explosives, to make a political point or to further a political cause.

One of the most famous images from the Vietnam War is that of a sixty-six-year-old Buddhist monk, Quang Duc, who committed suicide in 1963 by setting himself on fire in a busy intersection of what was then the South Vietnamese capital, Saigon (now Ho Chi Minh City). He was protesting the treatment of Buddhists by the South Vietnamese president, Ngo Dinh Diem.

This method of political protest was used more recently in Korea, in 1987, when two young men immolated themselves in separate incidents to protest the failure of opposition leaders to unite behind a single presidential candidate.

Then there are the suicide bombers. In an effort to achieve their political goals—for example, ending the political peace process between the Israeli government and the Palestine Liberation Organization—suicide bombers have used explosives to kill themselves and anyone within range of their deadly cargo. For more on politics and suicide, see chapter 1, "The Basics."

○ *How does desperation figure into the equation?*

We've all seen newspaper stories about people who try to kill themselves using a seemingly bizarre or desperate method. The sad fact is that those who feel desperate enough will use just about anything they can get their hands on to do the job.

Sometimes desperate methods work, as in the case of the politician I used to work for who grabbed a steak knife from the kitchen silverware drawer and stabbed himself in the heart. Suffering from severe depression over a bribery scandal in which he'd been implicated, he'd already tried to kill himself once. He was in his kitchen on the phone to his psychiatrist when he tried the second time, in what I can only imagine was a moment of desperation. His wife found him on the floor of the kitchen with a knife in his chest.

Sometimes people who are desperate use methods that don't work, as in the case of a clearly very desperate elderly man in a nursing home who tried chewing through his wrists late one night. He was found in his bed in the morning, bleeding but still alive.

Desperation sometimes results from a poorly planned and unsuccessful suicide attempt by someone who is emotionally distraught. Sherwin Nuland notes in *How We Die,* "In desperation, such people sometimes keep trying until they succeed, resulting in a body being discovered that has been lacerated, shot, and finally poisoned or hanged."

○ *Why do people who want to end their lives jump off bridges?*

People jump off bridges because they're there, just as people jump from tall buildings in places where there are tall buildings. But there's more: bridges are different. There's a sort of mystical or romantic appeal to the act of jumping off a bridge, as well as the potential for making a public statement. As Eve Meyer, at San Francisco Suicide Prevention, explained to me, "They get into the newspaper. By jumping off a bridge, they're able to make a statement that they couldn't make when they were alive. Then somebody else reads it in the newspaper and they think, *I can make a statement, too!*"

○ *Are some bridges more popular than others?*

Yes, in large part because some bridges are easier to jump off of than others. For example, the Golden Gate Bridge in San Francisco is accessible to pedestrians and has an easily scaled three-and-a-half-foot barrier between pedestrians and the water below. The nearby Bay Bridge, which carries vehicular traffic across San Francisco Bay from San Francisco to Oakland, has no pedestrian access and has far fewer jumpers. Also, some bridges, like the Golden Gate and the Brooklyn Bridge, have a greater mystical, romantic, and/or aesthetic draw than others.

○ *How many people have jumped from the Golden Gate Bridge? Has anyone survived?*

Since the Golden Gate Bridge opened in 1937, close to a thousand people are known to have jumped from it, but Eve Meyer believes the actual number is at least twice as high: "They find a lot more shoes and briefcases than bodies, but they only count the bodies."

Despite the more than 231-foot drop (from the highest point at low tide), cold water, and swift currents, approximately twenty people have survived, although almost all suffered significant injuries.

○ *Are there other places that have the same draw for people attempting suicide as the Golden Gate Bridge?*

Other than bridges, both the Empire State Building and the Eiffel Tower were a draw for people contemplating suicide

until barriers were constructed to prevent people from jumping off.

Japan had an equivalent high-rise draw in Tokyo. An article
in the January 1994 issue of *Harper's* magazine called "A Final
Exit for Japan's Generation X" told about a family of three that
jumped from the top of an apartment building, an event that
led to a series of suicides. "At one point, someone jumped
from the building every three days," the article went on to say.
In 1981, a fence was constructed around the roof and a suicide
hot line was installed, drastically reducing the number of suicide attempts.

CHAPTER 3

TEEN/YOUTH
SUICIDE

*I*s *youth suicide a big problem?*

With five thousand young people reportedly killing themselves each year, there's clearly a problem, especially when you consider that the real number of youth suicides—like the number of all suicides—is two to five times higher than what is reported. Even going by the five-thousand figure, suicide is the third-greatest cause of death among people fifteen to twenty-four years old (accidents and homicide are first and second, respectively). But, seen in the context of all people who take their lives, the rate of suicide among young people is in proportion to the percentage of young people in the general population.

The fact that young people commit suicide in proportion to their numbers in the general population was of no comfort to Carolyn, a mother of three whose seventeen-year-old son committed suicide. "When I was growing up, I didn't know anyone who even *tried* to commit suicide. Maybe it happened and families called it an accident . . . but suicide?"

When Carolyn's son became deeply depressed and started getting in trouble, suicide was still something that never crossed her mind. "My son had been in a lot of trouble emotionally and into drugs. He also had said things to me that should have caught my attention, but I didn't recognize that he was suicidal." Despite talking to a series of counselors, Carolyn's son apparently saw only one solution to his problems and shot himself in the head one afternoon in his bedroom. To learn more about the impact on Carolyn of her son's death, please see chapter 7, "Coping with the Suicide of Someone You Know."

○ *What's the difference between teen and youth suicide?*

It's all in the numbers. Statisticians and researchers divide people into different categories, so when it comes to talking about teen suicide, some people are referring to kids aged fifteen to nineteen, and others include those who are fifteen to twenty-four. Then there are the researchers who look specifically at college-age kids, the twenty-to-twenty-four crowd, and those who keep track of children aged ten to fourteen.

In this chapter, I generally answer questions about "youth" suicide, which covers people aged fifteen to twenty-four.

○ *What about children aged ten to fourteen? Don't some of them commit suicide?*

Though there are relatively few suicides in this age group—in comparison to those over the age of fourteen—such suicides increased by 120 percent overall between 1980 and 1992. Looking at the numbers in more detail, it turns out that the increase varies dramatically between boys and girls, and between blacks and whites. For white boys, the rate increased 86 percent, and for white girls, 233 percent. For black boys, the rate went up 300 percent, and for black girls, 100 percent.

○ *What happened?*

No one knows for sure, but there are some very educated guesses. For example, kids today are under even greater pressure at an earlier age, for reasons ranging from an increasingly fractured family life to greater violence in the communities where they live, so they're likely to experience more mental disorders, including depression. Add to that the ever increasing availability of guns and you have the volatile mix that leads to more completed suicides. The twelve-year-old who might have impulsively swallowed a handful of aspirin back in the 1970s and survived to talk about it can now send a final message to his friends and family by impulsively putting a bullet through his brain.

○ *Is youth suicide (suicide among those fifteen to twenty-four years old) also a growing problem?*

With all the headlines over the years about the "epidemic" of teen/youth suicide and how the numbers of these suicides have increased by 200 or 300 percent since the 1950s, you would think this was a growing problem, with dramatic increases each year in the number of youth suicides. That's what I thought, but that's not what the statistics show. The annual number of reported suicides among youths fifteen to twenty-four years old is around five thousand, a number that has been stable or has decreased slightly since the late 1970s.

○ *What about the big increase in the number of reported youth suicides?*

In fact, there was a big increase—more than 200 percent—in the number of reported youth suicides between the 1950s and the late 1970s, but as usual, not every expert on this subject can agree on the reasons for this increase. Here are some of the reasons I came across:

○ The increase in numbers is a result of the greater willingness of coroners to state the true cause of death. For example, coroners are less likely today to report a suicide from a gunshot wound as an accidental death than they were years ago.

○ The rise was caused by a combination of family disintegration and the social and economic dislocation that goes along with it, greater competition for jobs, the increasing availability of guns, and the influence of movies, television programs, and rock music with violent and suicidal themes.

○ The increase resulted from a decline in church attendance, coupled with high divorce rates and high unemployment. The theory here is that with fewer young people receiving religious instruction, they're less likely to view suicide as a sinful act, and that without religious faith they are less able to get through difficult times.

I think all three of these explanations make good points, although to greater or lesser degrees. I'm willing to bet that the changing attitudes of coroners and the increasing availability of guns were the biggest factors in the increase in reported youth suicides, followed by a combination of family disintegration, declining religious faith, and greater economic challenges. Given all of these very significant factors, I suspect that movies, television, and rock music played a negligible role if any in the increase in reported youth suicides.

○ *What accounts for the stable or slight decrease in the total number of reported youth suicides since the late 1970s?*

Well, if you don't really know for sure what caused the dramatic increase in the first place, it's hard to say why the numbers of youth suicides have remained about the same for years. Certainly no one is going to argue that the consistent number of reported youth suicides is a result of more stable family life. If anything, family life is more chaotic today than it was in the late 1970s. And guns are more available than ever.

Maybe the answer is that there's a greater willingness to talk about problems in general, so that young people have more freedom to discuss what's bothering them and don't feel compelled to follow through on suicidal feelings. And perhaps suicide-prevention programs are making a difference. But whatever the reasons, the good news is that youth suicide is not a growing problem. The bad news, of course, is that thousands of young people are still killing themselves each year and leaving behind many thousands of distraught, grief-stricken, and guilt-ridden loved ones.

○ *How many young people attempt suicide each year?*

It depends on whom you ask, but the estimates range from two hundred thousand a year to 2 million or more.

○ *Is there a difference in suicide rates between male and female youth?*

Yes, just like their adult counterparts, more young men than young women commit suicide. Roughly, of the five thousand young people who commit suicide each year, eight hundred are female. But far more young women attempt suicide than do young men. Although no one really knows how many people attempt suicide, experts on the subject generally agree that young women make three times as many suicide attempts as young men. Young men are far more likely to complete a suicide.

○ *Is there a difference in the rate of suicide between young people from affluent families and those from economically disadvantaged families?*

No. Marsha Alterman, the director of TeenLine, a crisis line for young people located in Charleston, South Carolina, says that in this regard, suicide among youth is "an equal opportunity killer."

○ *Why do young people attempt or commit suicide?*

Why would two seemingly happy, academically successful girls from apparently happy homes lie down in front of a moving train and end their lives? Why would a sensitive, lovable fourteen-year-old boy hang himself from a tree in his backyard? Why would a talented, peaceful college student use a gun to kill herself?

There is generally no one reason a young man or woman decides to commit suicide. Even if you can point to something, like the breakup of a relationship or a fight with parents, that may indeed be the incident that triggered the suicide or suicide attempt, there's almost always more to it than that. And in all likelihood, the suicide had been contemplated for quite some time.

Virginia tried to kill herself during her third year of college by putting her head in the oven of the off-campus apartment she shared with two of her classmates. It was something she'd been thinking about for years. "I'd been depressed since even before college and always spent a lot of time alone in my room, lighting candles and reading a lot of Sylvia Plath and Virginia Woolf. I was sure I'd die before I was twenty-four, like Keats. I had this romantic image of myself as a poet and as a doomed person. At some point the image got carried away. I decided to follow Sylvia Plath's example, and she killed herself by putting her head in her oven and turning on the gas. No one told me that it was a different kind of gas in her day, and that it was very difficult to kill yourself with the gas we use now."

Before her suicide attempt, Virginia found herself sinking into a deeper and deeper depression, and she spent increasing amounts of time alone. "I look back now and can see that I really withdrew from my friends. I had no one to talk to, except for my boyfriend, and when he decided to end our relationship because I didn't have the kind of background his parents would approve of, that just pushed me over the edge." For more information about Virginia's suicide attempt and its aftermath, please see chapter 5, "Attempted Suicide."

Everyone's story is different, so trying to understand why a young person attempts or commits suicide is not easy. And sometimes it's simply impossible to understand why, because the young person takes his reasons with him. But in the broadest sense, the young people who try to kill themselves are those who are unable to cope with the challenges of life and become overwhelmed. They lose hope and, seeing no way out of their despair, choose suicide as their only option.

For Collin, who is now in his final year of college, his suicide attempt at age fifteen had a lot to do with his demanding parents. "I used to fantasize about killing myself as a way of getting back at them. But what finally made me do it for real was when I got a 'D' on my math exam in tenth grade. I got home from school and I went to my mother's medicine cabinet and swallowed a bunch of different pills."

Grades were a sore subject around Collin's house. "My parents never gave me any slack. They're both really smart academically, but I always had to work extra hard just to keep a 'B' average." A year before the attempt, Collin's parents hired a tutor. "It didn't help raise much except their expectations of me. Whenever I came home with my report card, I could count on a tongue-lashing or punishment of some kind for every grade below a 'B.' After a while, I felt like I was nothing. And then I got that 'D,' and I thought my parents were going to kill me, so I figured I'd save them the trouble and do it myself. I didn't see any other way out."

Following is a list of general reasons why young people commit suicide. Those who follow through on suicidal thoughts usually have several things going on in their lives at the same time that have collectively pushed them to make the desperate choice of killing themselves.

- Depression or other mental illness, which may lead to feelings of helplessness and hopelessness and, ultimately, to thoughts of suicide.
- The breakup of a relationship or conflicts with parents.

- Feelings of isolation, of being different.
- An impulsive reaction over a short-term disappointment (e.g., a high achiever who has a setback). Unlike adults, young people don't have the experience to know that every crisis or defeat isn't permanent.
- A sense of personal worthlessness.
- Failure or fear of failure.
- Problems with drug and/or alcohol abuse.
- An unwanted pregnancy.
- Parental divorce or family instability.
- Sexuality conflicts.
- Reports of other suicides.
- A history of suicide in the family, which can lead a young person to think of suicide as a reasonable way of coping with problems. Also, a history of suicide in the family may mean a history of depression, which can lead to suicide.

○ *Which young people are most at risk of committing suicide?*

The odds are that an emotionally stable young woman from a happy, intact home who is doing reasonably well in school is unlikely to have suicidal thoughts. However, if a young man has problems with depression, comes from a chaotic single-parent household, has few friends, and has attempted suicide before, there is great risk that he will complete a suicide.

Other major risk factors include everything from mental illness and an inability to discuss problems with parents to the recent breakup of a relationship, problems with drugs, and the death of a family member.

○ *Are there warning signs?*

After her son's suicide, Carolyn read everything she could about suicide and discovered that there had been warning signs that she never picked up on. Determined that this would never happen to her other children, she kept a close eye on them for any signs of trouble. "I just about drove them crazy, because a lot of the signs are the kinds of things you might expect from any young person, suicidal or not—from problems with school to bad moods."

Not every moody or depressed young adult is suicidal. Nor is every high school student who suddenly starts getting bad grades necessarily thinking about ending his life. But it's important to pay close attention to moody or depressed young people, and to the following warning signs:

○ Talking about wanting to die or making suicidal threats.

○ Problems in school, at work, or with the police.

○ Withdrawal from friends and/or family.

○ A sudden change in personality and/or behavior.

○ Giving things away, especially prized possessions.

○ A significant change in sleep patterns or eating habits.

○ A sudden lack of energy and/or enthusiasm for friends and activities.

○ More aggressive and impulsive behavior (e.g., violent outbursts).

○ A history of physical or psychological illness.

○ Running away.

○ An unwanted pregnancy.

○ Drug and/or alcohol abuse.

- Rejection by a boyfriend or girlfriend.
- The recent suicide of a friend or relative.
- A sudden and extreme neglect of appearance.
- An obsession with songs, poems, books, or movies with suicidal themes.
- Previous suicide attempt(s).

This list is obviously very broad, and the vast majority of teenagers and young people who exhibit almost any of these behaviors—alone or in various combinations—don't attempt or complete a suicide. But some do, and because of that possibility it's important to pay attention, listen, and, if necessary, get help.

○ *How much of a factor is drug and/or alcohol use?*

Alcohol especially is a significant factor. More than half of all adolescent suicides and suicide attempts are associated with alcohol. In other words, the person who attempts or commits suicide has often been drinking immediately prior to the attempt.

○ *Does rock music lead teenagers to commit suicide?*

Rock music does not lead teenagers to commit suicide. But if your child or friend is obsessed with songs of any kind that deal with suicide, you have reason to be concerned, because this could mean he or she is having thoughts of suicide.

○ *How much of a factor is the availability of firearms?*

Guns are a huge factor and can turn an adolescent cry for help into a final act of desperation. For young people especially, whose suicidal feelings may be sudden and short-lived, guns provide a very permanent solution to often temporary problems.

A *Newsweek* article about teen suicide that followed the death of rock star Kurt Cobain made note of a study comparing adolescent suicide victims who had no apparent mental disorders with kids who didn't commit suicide. The study found only one difference between the two groups: a loaded gun in the house.

○ *How much of a factor is sexual orientation?*

Conflicts over sexual orientation can be a big factor. Young people who are wrestling with sexual-identity issues face a range of problems that, combined with the usual challenges of growing up, increase their risk of choosing suicide as a solution. Sometimes the conflict is over antigay religious beliefs or societal condemnation. At other times the conflicts involve parents and/or family members who reject or are hostile to their gay or lesbian child or relative. Gay and lesbian young people may also face taunts and physical abuse from classmates at school. And they may have no place to turn for help. So they suffer in relative isolation, unable to share with anyone what they're going through.

When Bonnie was fifteen, she told her parents she was gay. Her parents had gay friends and her mother was a psychologist, so Bonnie knew they weren't going to throw her out of the house. And she felt fairly certain that they would be okay about it. "It was making me crazy, hiding it from them, because we talked about everything. I'm an only child, so I always got a lot of attention. What finally pushed me to tell them was that I had a crush on one of my classmates and I needed to talk to someone about it, so I decided to tell my parents about it one evening over dinner."

Bonnie's parents gave no hint of shock as she described her crush on another girl and told them she was gay; dinner proceeded without anyone skipping a beat. "My parents did a good job of listening and, I think, had pretty good advice about how to handle my crush. But as we were doing the dishes, my mother calmly explained to me how learning about the fact I was a lesbian was like experiencing a death for them and that they'd need some time to get used to it. I was stunned."

What Bonnie's mother was trying to do was explain how she felt, but that wasn't the way Bonnie heard it. "I found out later that this was my mother's way of trying to let me know that they were having a hard time with this but that they still loved me. At the time, the way I heard it, they were telling me that I was dead to them. I was so upset and felt so rejected that I didn't know what to do."

That night, after her parents had gone to sleep, Bonnie decided to "punish" her parents. "I decided to teach them a lesson and show them what it would be like for me to be really dead. I felt like a robot as I went downstairs to the kitchen and got my mother's favorite paring knife, sat down at the kitchen table, and started cutting. Thank God my mother heard me in the kitchen, because I hadn't done that much damage by the time she walked in. Still, I was bleeding from the cuts, and my parents rushed me off to the emergency room."

○ *Is it true that a third of all teen suicides are gay or lesbian?*

This is a number that's been tossed around so often that it is almost taken as fact. But it's not. Various studies over the years have shown that gay and lesbian young people (as well as adults) are at higher risk of suicide, but there is no conclusive evidence that as many as a third of all the young people who commit or attempt suicide are gay or lesbian.

○ *Are there places where gay and lesbian young people can go to get help?*

Most major cities have support groups for gay and lesbian youth (as well as for bisexual and transgender youth). These groups can be found by calling the local gay and lesbian hot line or gay community center. A relative handful of high schools have counselors specifically trained to deal with sexual-minority issues. And many, if not most, colleges and universities have gay/lesbian/bisexual organizations, and counselors who are familiar with and sensitive to sexual-identity issues. Kids who are on-line can also make use of gay and lesbian computer bulletin boards and chat rooms available on the Internet as well as a number of commercial on-line services.

One organization I highly recommend for sexual-minority youth is the Hetrick-Martin Institute in New York City (see the listing in the appendix). Hetrick-Martin provides professionally trained staff counselors who can talk with you by phone and/or provide referrals to resources in your community.

○ *Does publicity of a youth suicide — or suicides — lead others to do the same?*

For some young people who are already depressed and inclined to be self-destructive, learning about the suicide of someone whose situation they perceive to be like theirs may provoke them to do what they've already imagined doing.

Even that possibility should give sensationalistically inclined newspaper and television reporters, producers, and editors pause when they think about playing up the latest family tragedy in some suburban neighborhood or affluent community where these things aren't supposed to happen.

For example, in late 1994, in a small community in Indiana, a female high school student committed suicide using a gun. The incident was widely publicized, with plenty of headlines in the local press. Two days later another high school student in a nearby community put a gun to his head and ended his life. When I asked a neighbor of the second student whether he thought this was just a coincidence, he said, "No way. In a place where this kind of thing only happens once every five years or so, it's hardly a coincidence when two high school students shoot themselves to death within days of each other. I think the local newspapers have to take some responsibility for this, although I realize it might have happened even if they'd kept the story off the front page."

This is not a new issue. Researchers on the subject often cite the case of an eighteenth-century romantic novel that was blamed for leading impressionable young people to commit suicide. The book, Johann Wolfgang von Goethe's *The Sorrows of Young Werther*, published in 1774, tells the story of an artistic young man who shoots himself in the head. Various European governments responded by banning the sale of the book or forbidding its publication.

We can't pretend that youth suicide doesn't happen. And when it happens, the public certainly needs to be made aware of it, along with information that can help prevent other suicides. Fortunately, some news organizations report these tragedies responsibly. But others don't, and screaming headlines and sensationalistic television news anchors don't help anyone and may in fact push one more depressed and alienated kid over the edge.

○ *What is a suicide cluster?*

When one suicide triggers others over a period of days or weeks, this is called a *suicide cluster*. Sometimes the phrase *copycat suicide* is also used in these circumstances. Clusters and copycat suicides most often, but not always, involve youth.

When the rock singer Kurt Cobain committed suicide in April 1994, there was plenty of speculation in the media as to whether this would lead to a series of copycat suicides among Cobain's youthful fans. It never happened. In writing about the fallout from Cobain's suicide, *Newsweek* noted that "while there was one apparent copycat suicide, by a 28-year-old man who attended the candlelight vigil and then went home and shot himself, most of Cobain's fans seem to have mourned him without endorsing his suicide."

○ *What should you do if you think a young friend or your child is suicidal?*

What you should specifically do depends on the circumstances, but two general things are key: listen, and get help.

The first thing you need to do is listen. For one thing, it's not always clear when someone is having suicidal feelings or thoughts. Even if your friend or loved one is in fact talking about feeling suicidal, he or she may express this in a way that's ambiguous, only hinting at suicide. For example, he or she may talk about wanting to "disappear," or not wanting to "go on," or feeling like "giving up." If you're not sure what you're hearing, you can ask, "Have you been thinking about suicide?" If the answer is yes, ask why, and then listen.

It may be tempting to dismiss your friend's or loved one's thoughts and feelings by telling that person he or she is just being foolish or that things will be okay tomorrow. Don't do it, because then you probably won't get the chance to hear what's bothering your friend or loved one. And you won't have the chance to help.

Helping may involve no more than offering to go with your friend or loved one to a school guidance counselor to talk out how he or she is feeling. If your friend or loved one won't go, you should take your concerns to someone you know who will show an interest in this person—a guidance counselor, clergy person, or family member.

Even if the suicidal young person has sworn you to secrecy, this is one case where it's okay to break your promise and get help. It's better to have a friend who is mad at you than one who is dead.

In the event your friend or loved one seems to be in imminent danger of hurting himself or herself, call for emergency help *immediately*.

○ **What is being done to prevent teen/youth suicide?**

Plenty, from high school programs designed specifically to reduce teen/youth suicide to special training for school counselors and teachers so that they can recognize students who are potentially suicidal. For more on this subject, see chapter 6, "Treatment and Prevention."

○ **How do people react to the suicide of a teenager?**

Suicide almost always leaves family and friends devastated and bewildered. When the person who commits suicide is young, the devastation can be even more extreme and the bewilderment even more overwhelming. How, we wonder, could someone whose whole adult life was ahead of him or her end it before it had even begun? For more on this subject, see chapter 7, "Coping with the Suicide of Someone You Know."

○ *Can you recommend any books on teen/youth suicide?*

I've listed a number of books on this subject in the appendix.

CHAPTER 4

SUICIDE AND
THE ELDERLY

*H*ow big a problem is suicide
among the elderly?

Elderly people are more likely than people of any other age group to take their own lives. Although only about 12 percent of the population is elderly, they account for approximately 20 percent of all people who commit suicide.

○ *How many elderly people attempt suicide each year?*

Various experts estimate that among the elderly there are from two to four suicide attempts for every completed suicide. By comparison, for young people there are two hundred or more attempts for every completion.

If you accept the official figure of approximately six thousand suicides among the elderly each year, that means there are from twelve thousand to twenty-four thousand attempts annually. But if the true suicide rate is three to five times higher, as many as one hundred twenty thousand elderly people attempt suicide each year.

○ *What exactly do you consider elderly?*

I personally don't consider age sixty-five to be the dividing line between those who are elderly and those who are not, but that's how the statistics are calculated, and someone chose to call this group elderly. So for the purposes of this section, when I refer to the elderly, I'm talking about those people who are sixty-five years of age and older.

○ *Why are elderly people more likely to complete a suicide than other age groups?*

Elderly people are more likely to complete a suicide than those under sixty-five because when they decide to take their lives, they're very serious about it. Generally, these are not people making a cry for help or attempting to get back at a boyfriend or girlfriend. They want to die. They choose more lethal methods. And they get it right the first time. Many of them live alone, so even if their suicide attempt is a cry for help, they're far less likely to be found in time to be saved.

○ *What lethal methods are the elderly likely to use?*

The elderly are more likely to use firearms, although as in the general population, elderly men are more likely than women to use guns. Elderly women are more likely to use pills or poisons of some kind. Elderly people are also more likely to use self-starvation as a method of ending their lives or to choose to ignore a doctor's advice and/or stop taking essential medication, knowing that this is likely to kill them.

When Jeanne's father was in his late sixties, he was told by his doctor that he absolutely had to quit smoking, drop weight, and restrict his intake of sweets. "If he didn't," Jeanne said, "the doctor warned him that he was in grave danger." Jeanne's father did just the opposite of what his doctor instructed and even stopped taking his blood-pressure medication. "We had screaming arguments over what he was doing. I told him he was committing suicide, but he said life wasn't worth living if he couldn't smoke and couldn't eat what he wanted. What got me was that he didn't care that he was robbing his daughter of her only surviving parent and his grandchildren of their only grandfather. I thought he was being incredibly selfish, but I couldn't get through to him. Nobody could." Jeanne's father died eleven months later. "The death certificate said it was a stroke, but I thought it should have said 'suicide.'"

○ *Why do elderly people attempt or commit suicide?*

Elderly people commit suicide for many of the same reasons younger people do. But for the elderly, the reasons more frequently include ill health, chronic pain, fear of burdening children, economic problems, death of a spouse, and loneliness. All of these factors can also contribute to depression and/or a loss of hope.

As with all people, when the elderly decide to take their own lives, most often there isn't one thing that you can point to as *the* reason. There may be one reason you can cite as the trigger, but once you take a closer look, you're likely to find other contributing factors.

For Ruth, who was in her mid-eighties at the time of her suicide attempt, a severe back injury was the final straw. "Since my husband died, walking and ballroom dancing were the two things that saved me." Even during the deep depression that followed her husband's death, Ruth still walked three miles every day, and after a year of mourning she returned to ballroom dancing. "It wouldn't have been right to go back any sooner."

For all of her life, Ruth had enjoyed good health. "I'd always taken care of myself, watched my diet, took vitamins, so I never expected to have problems." Three crushed vertebrae, the result of a fall, left Ruth in great pain and unable to dance at all or walk more than a few blocks at a time. "I didn't want to see anyone or talk to anyone. I even stopped answering the phone. I had friends, but I shut them out. I was too embarrassed for them to see me in my condition. If I couldn't be myself anymore, I just wanted to die."

Ruth decided to take matters into her own hands, and one evening, after straightening her apartment and putting on a fresh nightgown, she swallowed a bottle of painkillers. "I was so angry when I woke up in the hospital," she said. A neighbor, concerned after knocking at Ruth's door and not getting an answer, had called the building's superintendent. They had found Ruth on her sofa, unconscious but still breathing.

○ *Are there differences in the suicide rate between the "young" elderly and the "old" elderly?*

Yes. The older people are, the more likely they are to kill themselves.

○ *Is suicide among the elderly a growing problem?*

The rate of suicide among the elderly is currently stable, but at one time suicide among the elderly was a far greater problem. In 1933, for example, the suicide rate among the elderly was more than two times what it is today.

○ *What accounts for the overall decrease since the 1930s?*

Unfortunately, no one really knows for sure, because surprisingly little attention has been paid to the subject of suicide and the elderly. But among the possible reasons are improved medical care, pension programs, and the introduction of Social Security and various government programs for the elderly. As difficult as life can be for the elderly, it is far better today than it was a few decades ago.

○ *Is there a difference in suicide rates between male and female elderly people?*

There's an enormous difference in the rate of suicide between men and women in general. It's even greater among the elderly, and that difference increases with age.

Among people of all ages, the rate of suicide for men is about 20 per 100,000 and for women it's about 5 per 100,000. For elderly men, the rate is about 42 per 100,000, and for elderly women it's about 6.5 per 100,000. Another way of looking at this is to say that for every ten elderly women who kill themselves, approximately sixty-four elderly men take their lives.

After age sixty-five, the rate of suicide for women decreases gradually to 5 per 100,000 for those eighty-five years of age and older. But for elderly men, the rate of suicide increases significantly over the years, to 60 per 100,000 for those eighty-five years of age and older. (These numbers are drawn from "Epidemiology of Suicide in the Elderly," by Dr. John L. McIntosh, published in the spring 1992 edition of *Suicide and Life-Threatening Behavior*.)

○ *What about marital status? Does that make a difference?*

Marital status among the elderly has a huge impact. Married people have the lowest risk of suicide, and divorced and widowed people have the highest rates of suicide. Those who were never married fall between the two groups.

· Elderly men are more affected by marital status than elderly women. The suicide rate for married elderly men is about 32 per 100,000. For widowed elderly men it's more than two and a half times that amount. And the suicide rate for divorced elderly men is more than triple the rate for married men.

For married elderly women the suicide rate is approximately 5 per 100,000. For widowed elderly women the rate is about 8. And for divorced elderly women the rate is around 13. (These numbers are also drawn from the McIntosh article mentioned above.)

Following the death of my mother's mother, Grandma Ethel, my grandfather threatened to kill himself. Grandpa had been devoted to Grandma, and over the years, as his memory failed, she watched out for him like a hawk. They ran an old gift shop together, and were never apart for more than a few moments.

Because Grandpa needed twenty-four-hour care, after Grandma's death my mother had to move him into a nursing home. The first three times my mother and I went to visit him, Grandpa asked where Grandma was and Mom explained to him that she had died. Each time, he greeted the news with shock, grief, and threats that he was going to kill himself. All he could manage to say was "No Ethel?" And then in a rage he repeatedly ran his finger across his neck in a motion suggesting that he was cutting his throat. We felt confident that with twenty-four-hour care he wouldn't be a real danger to himself, but it broke our hearts to see the pain he was in.

After the third visit, Mom decided to use Grandpa's compromised memory to spare him the news of Grandma's death. When he asked where Grandma was, she simply said that Grandma would be arriving shortly. He accepted that explanation and then promptly forgot he had ever asked. Believing that his Ethel was still alive, Grandpa never again threatened to kill himself.

○ *Why do elderly white men have the highest rate of suicide?*

In general, elderly white men have the furthest to fall both economically and socially as they age. They are also less likely to have a strong support network, and they are far less likely to ask for help.

○ *Why do elderly black women have a very low rate of suicide?*

I have tried to avoid generalizations, but here is another. Black women, in comparison to white men, are more likely to have been tempered by a lifetime of coping with adversity. Their status within society does not decline with age. And they're far more likely to have a strong support network.

○ *How can you tell if an elderly person is at risk for suicide? Are there warning signs?*

For anyone with even a little experience with elderly suicide, it was obvious that Ruth was in danger of killing herself in the months following her accident. She withdrew from her friends. She met with an attorney to get her will updated. And she gave away a few of her favorite possessions to her niece and a couple of her young friends. But even to those close to her, everything Ruth did made perfect sense in the context of what was going on in her life and the kind of person she was. She had every reason to be depressed over her circumstances. And given how practical she'd always been, there was nothing really suspicious about her wanting to have her will in order. Giving away some of her favorite possessions should have been the tip-off, but even that didn't raise any eyebrows, because it seemed like the practical thing to do at her age. Of course, everything Ruth did also made perfect sense for someone who was planning to commit suicide.

In addition to the general signs to watch out for in all people who may be suicidal, when it comes to the elderly, it is important to pay special attention to the following:

- Talk of wanting to die.
- A reduced interest in favorite activities and hobbies.
- Depression.
- Giving away treasured possessions.
- Reworking or preparing a will.
- Acquiring the means (e.g., buying a gun, saving medication, etc.).

○ *Is loneliness a big risk factor?*

Yes. Loneliness and the lack of a social network are factors in suicide in general, but for older people, who often have a smaller or nonexistent social network because of the deaths of their peers, loneliness is an even greater contributor to suicidal feelings.

○ *Which elderly people are most at risk of committing suicide?*

Broadly speaking, elderly people who are most at risk are older (seventy-five-plus) white men who have debilitating medical conditions, are suffering from depression, are widowed, divorced, or single, lack strong religious faith, and are without a supportive social network. Of course, most people who fit this profile never attempt suicide, but those who do fit it are most at risk.

○ *Are family and friends more likely to ignore suicidal signs in an elderly person?*

Yes. Most people don't think there's anything all that odd about an old person talking about wanting to die, being depressed, or tying up loose ends. Depending on the circumstances, we just think of such behavior as a normal response to old age.

○ *Is it harder for doctors to detect suicidal signs in an older person than in a younger person?*

Unless the doctor is specifically trained to deal with the elderly, yes. That's because the elderly are less likely than younger people to talk about their problems. And when they do, the doctor may simply assume that talk of being depressed or wanting to die just goes along with old age.

○ *How common is it for elderly couples to commit suicide? Why do they do it?*

It happens only a handful of times each year, but these kinds of suicides—murder-suicides or dual suicides—are generally so heartbreaking that we're sure to hear about them on the news or read about them in the newspaper.

Typically what happens in these cases is that an elderly couple faced with ill health decide to end their lives together. Or the spouse who has been taking care of his ailing wife, for example, becomes ill himself and, fearing that he won't be able to take care of his wife, decides to kill her and himself.

One story I came across, reported by the Associated Press in October 1983, was about Julia and Cecil Saunders of North Fort Myers, Florida. Julia, eighty-one, and Cecil, eighty-five, had been married for sixty years, and until Mrs. Saunders was placed in a nursing home in early 1983, they were rarely apart.

The AP reported, "Mrs. Saunders's dimming eyesight, heart congestion and a stroke had driven her husband to place her in a nursing home. . . . But she became hysterical over what she thought was poor care there, and Mr. Saunders took her home."

Three weeks later, they laid out the clothes they planned to be buried in, had lunch, and "drove to a rural corner of Lee County and parked. As cows grazed in the summer heat, Cecil Saunders shot his wife . . . in the heart and turned the gun on himself."

The note they left read: "Dear children, this we know will be a terrible shock and embarrassment. But as we see it, it is one solution to the problem of growing old. We greatly appreciate your willingness to try to take care of us.

"After being married for 60 years, it only makes sense for us to leave this world together because we loved each other so much.

"Don't grieve because we had a very good life and saw our two children turn out to be such fine persons. Love, Mother and Father."

The police sergeant who investigated the murder-suicide was struck by "how considerate, how thoughtful they were to all concerned about killing themselves." As reported in the story: "On the floorboard of the car, Cecil and Julia Saunders had placed typewritten funeral instructions, including the use of the clothes they had laid out, and the telephone numbers of their son and daughter. They draped the Chevrolet's seat with a shower curtain and wool blanket so their blood would not stain the car."

○ *What should you do if you think an elderly person is suicidal?*

Talk about it. In a caring and concerned manner ask, "Have you been having suicidal thoughts?" Some people think that by asking a person if he or she is suicidal you will either encourage the act or plant the idea. This is a myth. According to Dr. Daniel A. Plotkin, a Los Angeles geriatric psychiatrist who helped me with several of the previous questions, "When it's brought up, it's a relief to the person contemplating suicide. It doesn't push them over the edge."

The next step after talking about it is to get help. If the danger doesn't appear imminent, there's time to suggest that your friend or family member talk to his or her primary-care physician. If the person refuses, talk to the physician yourself and ask what you should do next.

You can also suggest that the person see a psychologist or psychiatrist, but then you may get into the problem of perceptions. Many older people have the idea that only crazy people go to psychologists or psychiatrists. Dr. Plotkin has run into this problem on more than one occasion with family members who come to him asking how they can get their elderly relative to agree to see him. "I tell them to tell their relative that I'm a geriatric specialist. That way the relative won't think anyone is telling them they're crazy."

Unfortunately, there isn't always time to arrange for a visit with a doctor. If the danger seems imminent, call a suicide hot line or 911 — and don't leave your friend or loved one alone.

○ **What can be done to help an elderly person who is suicidal?**

Elderly people who are suicidal benefit from the same standard treatments as any other age group, from antidepressant medication to group therapy.

After her suicide attempt, Ruth was kept in the hospital for a week and then transferred to a psychiatric facility where she was treated for her depression with a combination of therapy and medication. "There are days when I wish they'd let me die," she said, "but most of the time I'm glad they didn't." For more information on treatment, see chapter 6, "Treatment and Prevention."

○ **What can be done to reduce suicide among the elderly?**

Some things are very practical and doable, like educating the public about the problem of elderly suicide. We should all know what to look out for. And without question, doctors and mental-health professionals need to be better trained to recognize and treat elderly people who are suicidal.

Then there are those things that are less practical and less doable, like changing our society so that older people feel more valued and have more opportunities to play a meaningful role in their communities. Changes like these would go a long way toward reducing the loneliness and hopelessness that contribute to the depression so many older people experience.

○ *What is likely to happen to the suicide rate among the elderly as baby boomers age?*

One line of thought is that the rate may very well stay the same but that the overall numbers will increase because the baby-boomer generation is larger than the generation that preceded it. But another possibility is that the rate will decrease because boomers are generally more comfortable talking about problems and don't share the same negative attitudes toward seeking psychological help as previous generations; one can only hope.

CHAPTER 5

ATTEMPTED
SUICIDE

Who *attempts suicide?*

Hundreds of thousands of people
attempt suicide each year. They come from all walks of life, all
age groups, ethnic and racial groups, and sexual orientations.
However, those who attempt suicide and live (as opposed to
those who complete a suicide) are far more likely to be
women—three times as many women as men attempt suicide—and young. Half of all people who attempt suicide are
under age thirty. (Colt, p. 96)

Much like those who are more likely to commit suicide,
those who attempt suicide tend to be isolated, suffer from

some kind of mental illness such as depression or schizophrenia, and have drug and alcohol problems. Widows and widowers are more likely to attempt suicide than coupled people; white people more likely than other racial groups; and doctors more likely than bus drivers.

○ *Are all suicide attempts the same?*

No. Whereas some people who attempt suicide want very much to die and choose the most lethal means available, lots of people aren't nearly so determined and choose methods that are less likely to result in death.

In his book *Suicide: The Forever Decision*, Paul G. Quinnett explains that counselors generally view suicide in three distinct categories: "First-degree suicide attempts are planned, deliberate, premeditated acts involving the most lethal means. Second-degree attempts are more impulsive, unplanned, and not as well thought out. Third-degree attempts are those in which the person deliberately puts himself in a dangerous situation in which he may die, but his intent is not so clear."

For example, someone walking through traffic on a busy street, hoping to be hit, would be making a third-degree attempt. Someone impulsively swallowing a bottle of sleeping pills after an argument with a girlfriend would be making a second-degree attempt. And an elderly man shooting himself after getting all his affairs together and writing farewell notes to all his children would be making a first-degree attempt.

A first-degree attempt is more likely to result in death, but there are plenty of people who are very ambivalent about wanting to die, make a third-degree attempt, and wind up dead. And there are people who are very clear about wanting to die, make a first-degree attempt, and survive.

○ *Why do people attempt suicide?*

People attempt suicide for a variety of reasons, from extreme depression to misdirected anger. Please see chapter 1, "The Basics," for a detailed answer to why people attempt and commit suicide.

○ *What are people thinking when they attempt suicide?*

Some people have very clear thoughts, some are confused, irrational, and/or angry, and others are in a trancelike state in which they aren't thinking about anything other than doing what they have to do to end their lives.

Peter was in his mid-forties when he climbed over the railing of his apartment terrace. Following months during which he sank into a deeper and deeper depression, he found himself staring fourteen stories down to the street below. "To this day, I can't remember what happened in the days leading up to that moment, except that I was in such pain that I wanted my life to be over. I can't even say that I was thinking anything when I climbed back over the rail to safety. I was on total autopilot, with my self-destructive feelings doing battle with my will to live."

Ruth, whom I introduced in chapter 4, "Suicide and the Elderly," had very clear thoughts as she swallowed the pills that she hoped would end her life. "I felt so relieved that it was going to be over. I'd lived long enough. I'd had a good life. And now I was miserable. Why should I have to go on?"

○ *What should you do if you've just attempted suicide?*

Get help. If you've injured yourself or taken an overdose, you need to get emergency medical attention. If you haven't physically harmed yourself, you still need to get help. You can start by calling a close friend or relative or your doctor and telling him or her what you've done. If you're afraid to tell anyone you know, call a local crisis/suicide telephone line. If you think you're still in imminent danger of harming yourself, make sure you aren't alone and/or get yourself to a hospital emergency room.

Follow-up care with someone who has had experience dealing with suicidal patients is critical. You and those around you may prefer to pretend the suicide attempt never happened, but ignoring your attempt and not seeking help will just increase the risk that you'll try it again. I can't say this often enough: Get help!

○ *What do you do if someone has just attempted suicide?*

The immediate goal in the aftermath of a suicide attempt is to keep your friend or loved one alive and to make certain he or she doesn't try to make another attempt. I answer this question at greater length in chapter 6, "Treatment and Prevention."

○ *What do you do if you get a phone call from someone who has attempted suicide?*

As I explain in detail in chapter 6, "Treatment and Prevention," the goal is to get help to that person as quickly as possible.

○ *How do people react when they fail in their attempt to commit suicide?*

People react in a variety of ways, from anger and embarrassment to fear and relief. People who attempt suicide may be angry at themselves because, as the Olympic diver Greg

Louganis says in his autobiography about his first suicide attempt when he was twelve, "I couldn't even get that right." They may also be angry at themselves for trying in the first place. Or they may be angry at others for preventing them from carrying out their plan.

Ruth was furious with her neighbor for calling the building superintendent after she didn't answer her neighbor's repeated and loud knocks at the door. They found Ruth unconscious from an overdose of painkillers. "I was so angry! I had everything planned. No one was supposed to come by until the next day, and I would have been gone by then. I know she meant well, but it took a long time for me to see it that way. I thought she ruined everything. How could I not be angry at her?"

Ruth was also terribly embarrassed about what she had done. "The way I grew up, suicide was an awful thing. You never talked about it. And now I had to face my family, and everyone knew. When they came to see me in the hospital, I couldn't look at them or talk to them. I thought I would die just from the embarrassment."

Following a suicide attempt, some people also experience great fear because they feel out of control, particularly if they've been hospitalized following the attempt. They may also be fearful of themselves for having tried in the first place. That was Virginia's experience the first time she tried to take her life, when she was in her third year of college. "I was terrified. On the one hand, there I was, walking through traffic, hoping a car or bus would hit me. But on the other hand, I was terrified of what I was doing. I knew I had to get to the hospital before I got myself killed, even though I wanted to die. But obviously I also wanted to live. I was a mess."

For Peter, once he climbed back over the railing of his terrace and hurled himself into a corner in his living room, his terror over what he'd almost done was combined with a tremendous sense of relief. "I was totally relieved that I was still alive, that I hadn't gone through with it. But I couldn't move. I was afraid that if I got out of that corner I might actually jump, so I stayed in there all night, just holding myself. When the sun finally came up, I managed to get to the phone and call one of my close friends to tell him what happened."

○ *How do people react to someone who has attempted suicide?*

People react in a variety of ways. Ideally, they'll react with concern and understanding, as did Peter's friends. He told me: "My best friend flew out to stay with me for several weeks. She'd been through a severe depression herself, and she knew what I was going through. She never pushed me to talk, she was just there to take care of me. And once I was ready to talk, she was a great listener. My business partner was also amazing. He picked up the slack and encouraged me to take as much time as I needed to get better."

Not everyone is so fortunate. When Ruth tried to kill herself, she wasn't the only one who was embarrassed. Her sister was so ashamed, she didn't come to visit her in the hospital. "I can't blame her. I was ashamed, too. But I wish she had come to visit. She was the one person that I wouldn't have turned away from." After Ruth got out of the hospital, her sister was so afraid she'd try again that she called her several times a day. "After two days, I said, 'Enough!' I told her that I wasn't going to try again but if she didn't stop calling me I'd start thinking about it. I thought that was funny—I still had my sense of humor—but she started to cry."

Other people react with anger—"How could you do that!" And not just family and friends. Sometimes people who have attempted suicide face hostile medical personnel and fellow

patients who are filled with contempt for someone who would intentionally try to end his or her life.

Perhaps the worst response is no response at all. Some people simply go into denial and pretend that nothing ever happened. They may think this is the least painful way of handling things, but in the long run, pretending that everything is okay helps no one.

○ *How can you help someone who has attempted suicide?*

Much depends on your relationship with the person who has attempted suicide and the shape he or she is in following the attempt, but if you're a close friend or family member, you can be supportive of the person's recovery in the short and long term. The key is to avoid making judgments, and to listen. If it's appropriate, talk to the mental-health professionals who are involved in caring for the person who has attempted suicide and find out how best you can be of help. Or ask your loved one or family member directly, "What can I do to help you?" You can also call a suicide/crisis telephone line, explain your specific circumstances, and ask what they think you can do to help.

When Virginia called her parents following her attempt to kill herself by putting her head in the oven and turning on the gas, they came immediately to pick her up and bring her home. "I didn't wait for them to ask me if I wanted to see a psychiatrist. Before we even got home, I told them I needed to see a shrink and asked them to find me one. By that evening they had found a psychiatrist and made an appointment for first thing the next morning. They drove me to the doctor's office and waited to take me home. They were really great with practical things, but I wish they had been more comfortable talking about why I was so depressed in the first place. But my parents were never comfortable talking about those things."

○ *Do people who attempt suicide once try again?*

Fortunately, most people who try to kill themselves once don't do it again. But approximately 10 percent of those who make a first attempt will eventually take their own lives. (Colt, p. 98)

○ *What happens to people who survive an attempt?*

Depending on the circumstances, someone who survives a suicide attempt may wind up in an emergency room, locked in a psychiatric hospital on a twenty-four-hour suicide watch, or at home in bed for a day or two with a very bad headache.

After initial treatment at the hospital for her suicide attempt, Ruth was transferred to the psychiatric unit of a private hospital. "Everyone was very nice to me, but I didn't like the idea of people watching me." After she left the hospital, Ruth made weekly visits to a psychiatrist who specialized in treating depression among older people.

Some people who attempt suicide are released following initial medical treatment. Others, like Ruth, are sent to psychiatric facilities where, depending upon the case, they may stay for observation and treatment for a period of days, weeks, or months. If you're believed to be in danger of making another suicide attempt, a judge can even place you in a hospital and force you to stay there against your wishes.

○ *Do people who attempt suicide suffer from any permanent injuries?*

Yes. Depending on the method of suicide chosen, some people suffer brain injuries, paralysis, nerve damage, scarred wrists, and disfigurement. Some are left so impaired that even if they want to attempt suicide again, they can't.

○ *Do people recover from an attempt?*

Absolutely, although overcoming despair and hopelessness can take quite a long time. For some people, a close encounter with self-destruction is a major—and ultimately positive—turning point in their lives. For Peter, it was a slow road back to feeling normal again, but after the night he spent curled up in the corner of his living room, there was never any doubt that he wanted to live. "It was a tremendous shock to me that I'd reached the point where I was standing on the edge of my balcony, with nothing between me and a fourteen-story drop. When the sun came up the next morning, I was so glad to be alive—that I hadn't taken that final step. No matter how bad I've felt on occasion since that time ten years ago, I've never regretted that I chose life over the abyss."

CHAPTER 6

TREATMENT
AND
PREVENTION

*C*an people who have suicidal
thoughts get over their self-
destructive feelings?

In general, yes. Most people whose
suicidal thoughts are casual and fleeting will in time stop feeling suicidal, and time may be all they need. For those whose
thoughts are not casual and fleeting, particularly if the suicidal
feelings are a result of severe depression, schizophrenia, or alcoholism, for example, professional help is essential.

Virginia, whom I introduced in chapter 3, "Teen/Youth Suicide," pulled out of her suicidal despair through a combination of medication, therapy with a caring psychiatrist, and the passage of time.

Virginia was frightened by what she'd tried to do and knew she needed help. "Apparently I still wanted to live, because I wanted to get to a psychiatrist. I never missed an appointment." That was the beginning of Virginia's long climb out of depression and away from her feelings of hopelessness and despair. She explained, "My psychiatrist was a big man, full of life. After the initial visit, he prescribed an antidepressant, and then I met with him twice a week for the first few months. Most of the time we just talked about what was going on in my life. I liked his sense of humor, and one time, after telling him about some of the books I'd been reading, mostly depressing novels and books by people like Virginia Woolf, he told me to stay away from writers who killed themselves."

In time, Virginia's depression began to lift. "It was such a relief, although I still wrestled with mild depression from time to time for years afterward. But I vowed it would never get that bad again. I decided I wasn't going to let myself get boxed in to the point where I felt there was no way out other than suicide."

○ *What kinds of treatments are available?*

People who are experiencing suicidal feelings are treated in a variety of ways depending on what their underlying problems are and whether they're in imminent danger of hurting themselves. Treatment can range from a course of therapy with a mental-health professional and antidepressant and mood-stabilizing medication to electroconvulsive therapy (shock treatment) and hospitalization.

○ *Are there people who have suicidal feelings who do not benefit from treatment?*

Yes, although a significant part of the problem is that people who are feeling suicidal don't always get proper treatment or the right combination of treatments. But there are some people who receive extensive treatment yet continue to feel suicidal. That was the case with Serena, a thirty-five-year-old professional who lives with her parents. "I'd been struggling with depression and self-destructive feelings for quite a long time, and my psychiatrist tried two different antidepressants. One seemed to do nothing, and the other made me feel even more suicidal. I tried suffocating myself with a plastic bag, but I couldn't go through with it. I called my doctor to tell him what I'd done, and he recommended hospitalization."

Initially, Serena was very relieved to be in the hospital, but she quickly felt overwhelmed by her lack of freedom. "I was put in a locked ward, and I was on suicide watch for two weeks. I had constant supervision. I couldn't even pee alone. Still, I managed to get my hands on a pair of scissors, but fortunately they were discovered before I could hurt myself."

Serena was in the hospital for two months. She had individual and group therapy, and her psychiatrist prescribed lithium, but her depression didn't get any better and she became anorexic. Finally her doctor recommended electroconvulsive therapy (ECT). "I was freaked out by even the idea of shock treatments, but I trusted my doctor and I knew that it could be an effective method of treatment for people with severe depression. I went for six ECT treatments, and they weren't good for me. They made me horribly suicidal, and I was put on suicide watch. On Christmas day I freaked out and had to be put in restraints, because I'd tried to kill myself."

Within several weeks, Serena was stabilized and her doctor recommended she be transferred to a long-term-care facility because she continued to have self-destructive feelings. Serena liked that idea, but her insurance had run out by then, so she returned home to her parents and began seeing a psychiatrist on an out-patient basis. "I'm on an antidepressant and mood stabilizer, and they've helped, but lately I've started feeling suicidal again. Fortunately I have a very supportive network of people in my life, so I'm not isolated. That gives me hope that I'll make it. But I'm afraid this may be a lifetime struggle no matter what drugs I take or how long I'm hospitalized."

○ *What should you do if you're feeling suicidal?*

Talk to someone about it—a friend, a parent, a teacher, your family physician. You may feel embarrassed or ashamed of your feelings, but you'll likely discover that you're not alone in having these feelings. Lots of people have had them.

If your suicidal thoughts aren't casual and short-lived, it isn't enough to simply share your feelings. You've got to talk to a counselor who has experience in helping people who have suicidal thoughts. Some people think it's enough to talk to their family physician and get a prescription for antidepressants, but many physicians aren't trained to deal with suicidal patients, so it's important to get a referral to someone who has that experience. One way to find help is to call a local crisis line, explain that you're having suicidal feelings, and ask for a referral.

Also, if you've reached the point where you've already acquired the means for killing yourself, like a gun or sleeping pills, get rid of them now and get help. If you keep these items around the house, you may be tempted to use them. Serena explained to me that for the first two months she was out of the hospital, she avoided keeping plastic bags in her home. "As long as they were there I was afraid I'd use them." Serena also strongly recommends not being alone when you're having suicidal feelings. "My friends have been wonderful over the years about having me stay over at their homes."

○ *What should you say to someone who has told you he or she is feeling suicidal?*

Rather than trying to figure out what to say, focus instead on listening and asking questions. The person who is talking to you about his or her self-destructive feelings has probably overcome a lot of fear and embarrassment to share these feelings, and one thing you can do is make that person feel comfortable about opening up. Also, you can encourage him or her to talk to a professional and can offer your help in finding someone. If you're not sure how to handle the situation, call a mental-health center or crisis telephone line and ask for advice on what to do.

If the person appears to be in imminent danger to himself or herself, get help immediately. Call a crisis center or local emergency services.

○ *What shouldn't you say?*

Forget the sunny platitudes. It doesn't help to say, "Cheer up! You have everything to live for." The person confiding in you will likely feel dismissed by such a remark. Again, the key is listening and drawing the person out. Whatever you say should be in the spirit of making that person feel comfortable enough to keep talking. For example, depending on the circumstances, you can say, "It must have been very hard for you to tell me about this" or "I'm really glad you felt comfortable enough to confide in me."

○ *What do you do if someone has tried to commit suicide?*

If you find someone who has attempted suicide but is still alive, there are a number of things you can do, depending upon the circumstances. If the person has inflicted physical harm, administer first aid and call for emergency help. If he or she has used gas or carbon monoxide, get the person into the fresh air, administer CPR if necessary, and call for help. If the person has swallowed pills or taken some other poisonous substance and is unconscious, turn the person on his or her side to prevent choking and call for emergency help to find out what to do next.

○ *What do you do if you get a telephone call from someone who has just attempted suicide?*

If you get such a phone call, make certain that emergency help can get to the person quickly. First, ask whether anyone else is with the person. If so, ask the caller to put that person on the line and tell him or her to call for emergency help. If no one else is there, find out the caller's telephone number and address, including the apartment number, and ask the person to unlock the door so emergency help can get to him or her in the event he or she loses consciousness. Then, armed with the information you have, call for emergency help.

○ *How can we prevent suicide?*

At first glance, preventing suicide is simple. We have to identify those people who are at risk of taking their lives and then
make certain they get proper treatment. That's easier said than
done, of course, for two primary reasons. First, it's not so easy
to identify all those at risk. And even when those who are at
risk are so identified, they may not get appropriate treatment.

○ *How can you tell if someone is suicidal?*

Contrary to what many people think, you *can* often tell when
someone is contemplating suicide. Though people who are
planning to kill themselves don't generally announce their intentions explicitly, there are usually warning signs.

As suicidologist Edwin S. Shneidman explains in "At the
Point of No Return," an article published in the March 1987
issue of *Psychology Today,* "About 80 percent of suicidal people give friends and family clear clues about their intention to
kill themselves. They give indications of helplessness, make
pleas for response and create opportunities for rescue."

Shneidman notes that there are three broad categories of
clues: verbal, behavioral, and situational. In other words, a
person may make a statement about not wanting to go on,
about going away, or about not being able to stand the pain
any longer. Several months before my father committed suicide, he told his brother on more than one occasion that if
things kept going the way they were, he didn't "want to go on."
He didn't say he planned to kill himself, but his words were
still a pretty good indicator of what he was thinking about. My
uncle was alarmed, but uncertain as to what to do.

In terms of behavior, according to Shneidman, the person who is planning to commit suicide may give away "prized possessions, such as a medical student giving away a valuable microscope." Or the person may suddenly prepare a will. He or she may also behave differently than normal, changing usual eating, sleeping, work, and sexual patterns.

Shneidman describes as situational clues "traumatic events in a person's life, such as illness, the breakup of a relationship or the death of a loved one."

Not everyone who expresses a desire to end life does so verbally. Donna, a full-time mother of two young daughters, got a letter from her mother in which she talked about her wish to die. "Mom had been in and out of the hospital for drug and alcohol problems for years, so it's not as if I hadn't thought about the possibility of her accidentally overdosing. But until that letter, it really hadn't occurred to me that she would actually kill herself. Well, maybe it crossed my mind, but I didn't want to think about it. And it wasn't even that she said, 'I'm going to kill myself,' but she talked about being tired and how she would go to bed at night wishing she wouldn't wake up in the morning. Wouldn't that scare you?"

○ *Can you give a detailed list of the warning signs?*

The following list is drawn from several different sources, particularly Rita Robinson's *Survivors of Suicide*. Keep in mind that most people exhibit some, or even many, of these warning signs at various points in their lives yet never go on to commit suicide. Others, however, do.

  ○ Threats of suicide (e.g., "I'm going to shoot myself," "I don't want to go on," etc.).

- Preoccupation with death, including talk of hopelessness, helplessness, and/or worthlessness.
- Previous suicide attempts.
- Depression.
- Trouble with school or work.
- Alcohol and/or drug abuse.
- Risk taking.
- Isolation: withdrawing from friends and family.
- Personality changes and/or odd behavior.
- Difficulty with sleeping, loss of appetite.
- Moodiness, including anger and crying.
- Giving away prized possessions.
- Getting one's life in order, including the preparation or changing of one's will.
- The sudden appearance of happiness and calmness after a period during which some of the characteristics listed above were present.

- *Is there anything a doctor can do to find out if someone is at risk of committing suicide?*

Absolutely. People who are experienced in treating those who are suicidal can assess risk by first conducting an interview with the person who is believed to be suicidal. The information from that interview is then used by the mental-health professional to assess whether the person is suicidal and, if so, the severity of the danger. Current assessment techniques are more an art than an exact science, but they are an important way to begin identifying some of the people who are at risk.

○ *Do teenagers exhibit the same warning signs as the general population?*

Teenagers and young people show many of the same warning signs, but there are some differences. Please see chapter 3, "Teen/Youth Suicide," for a more detailed answer.

○ *What about elderly people? Are the warning signs the same for them as for the general population?*

Elderly people are not likely to be taken as seriously as younger people when they talk about wanting to die or being tired and not wanting to go on. Too often, we simply dismiss such statements as normal for someone in the later stages of life. However, they are not normal and may in fact be a warning sign. Many of the other warning signs are the same as they are for people in general, but are also easy to overlook. Please see chapter 4, "Suicide and the Elderly," for a more detailed answer.

○ *What should you do if you think someone is suicidal?*

As soon as Donna finished reading her mother's letter, she called her family physician to ask her advice on what to do. After asking Donna several questions to assess whether her mother was in imminent danger of taking her life, the doctor suggested that Donna bring her mother in that afternoon to talk.

Donna's instinct to get professional help was absolutely on target. This is not something you can handle on your own, and you can't risk doing nothing, hoping the problem will go away.

Depending on the immediacy of the situation, you can call your doctor, a counselor, or a local suicide hot line and get advice on what you can do to help a person you think is suicidal. If you're dealing with someone who is on the verge of committing suicide—who is, for instance, perched on the balcony of a tall apartment building—call the police or 911 and explain the situation. Every locality has experts with experience in dealing with this kind of emergency

○ *What is currently being done to prevent suicide?*

All across the country people are involved in a variety of efforts to reduce the number of people who take their lives, from volunteer crisis telephone hot lines—there are hundreds of such lines—and education programs about the problem of suicide to the installation of barriers on bridges.

For example, the American Association of Suicidology sponsors National Suicide Prevention Week, which is carried out at the local level by crisis-intervention centers and community mental-health centers. The goal of this program is to bring attention to the issue of suicide, to educate the public regarding the warning signs and risk factors, and to make people aware of the help that's available. Typically, local groups run training sessions for mental-health professionals, do public speaking in schools and community centers, and send out press releases about suicide prevention to local media.

Another example is the work done by Suicide Prevention Resources, a nonprofit educational agency that serves the five boroughs of New York City. David L. Conroy is the executive director of this mostly volunteer organization, which he founded in 1988. He explained, "We give talks to students as well as social-service professionals about suicide prevention."

Conroy said he gives approximately 350 talks a year, 200 of which are to students. "I begin by asking them what kinds of things cause suicide. They come up with a pretty good list. Then I talk about what it's like to be suicidal, the warning signs, how to initiate contact with someone, about listening to the person talk about their troubles without criticizing, and doing something about it, like going to other people to get help." Conroy said that inevitably after a presentation a handful of students will approach him to talk about someone they know who they believe is suicidal. "I help break the stigma so they can talk about it. And then I can arrange for school counselors to get involved."

Before founding Suicide Prevention Resources, Conroy was a volunteer for a suicide hot line and left the hot line to focus on education. He explained, "I wanted to get away from the notion of suicide prevention as a crisis situation. I want to reach the situation long before it reaches a crisis." Conroy still thinks hot lines are an important resource. "What happens on a hot line can be very helpful to the person. They can be lonely and despairing, and they get a sympathetic listener and can get connected with helpful agencies. The flaw with hot lines is that they reach only a tiny percentage of the population at a late date with a limited service."

○ *What exactly is a suicide hot line?*

Sometimes they're called suicide-prevention lines, crisis lines, or suicide hot lines, but typically these are telephone numbers that people who are in a crisis of some sort and/or are feeling suicidal can call at any hour of the day or night. The telephones are staffed by volunteers who have been trained to provide an empathetic ear and to refer callers to the appropriate agencies for further help.

One of the first volunteer-staffed suicide-prevention lines was founded in San Francisco in 1962 and is run by San Francisco Suicide Prevention. Eve R. Meyer, the executive director of the organization, explained how the suicide-prevention line is run: "We provide very intensive training to ordinary community people to handle crisis telephone calls. They come in once a week for four hours to answer phones. We have two hundred volunteers and get over two hundred telephone calls a day. When someone calls, we just listen, listen, listen like a vacuum cleaner. Most of them haven't had anyone to listen to them in a long time, which is why they're suicidal."

○ *Who calls?*

All kinds of people call, from distressed teenagers with relationship trouble to chronically depressed adults who need someone to talk to. But, according to Dr. Herbert Hendin, as he explains in his book *Suicide in America,* "the overwhelming number of calls and contacts do not come from the seriously suicidal segment of the population."

○ *Do suicide/crisis hot lines make a difference? Do they reduce the rate of suicide?*

Yes, suicide/crisis hot lines do make a difference in the lives of some of the people who call and perhaps reduce the numbers of people who attempt suicide. But in terms of actually reducing the numbers of people who commit suicide, the studies that have been done generally conclude that suicide/crisis hot lines do not have an impact on suicide rates.

○ *Does restricting access to guns keep people from killing themselves? Don't people just find other ways to do it?*

Common sense suggests that if a person wants to kill himself or herself and a gun or other convenient method of self-destruction isn't readily available, he or she will find another way to do it. And for someone intent on suicide, that may by exactly what he or she does. But suicide is often an impulsive act, and if a loaded gun is not nearby when the impulse is strongest, by the time another means can be found the impulse may have passed. If alcohol is involved, by the time another method is found the suicidal person may be more sober and therefore less inclined to kill himself or herself. It's also possible that whatever alternative method is chosen may not be as lethal.

This isn't just idle theory. As I mentioned in chapter 3, a *Newsweek* article about teen suicide that followed the suicide of the rock star Kurt Cobain made note of a study comparing adolescent suicide victims who had no apparent mental disorders with kids who did not commit suicide. The study found only one difference between the two groups: a loaded gun in the house.

○ *Has anything been done to prevent people from jumping off the Golden Gate Bridge?*

The pedestrian walkway has been closed at night in an effort to reduce the number of jumpers, and television cameras on the span allow bridge employees to keep a watchful eye out for potential suicides. When a potential suicide is spotted, the California Highway Patrol can reach the person within one minute and restrain him or her. Emergency telephones have also been installed on the span so that potential jumpers can call for help.

○ **Why haven't protective barriers been erected on the Golden Gate Bridge to prevent people from jumping off?**

This debate has raged for years, but the pro-barrier advocates have always lost out to those who oppose them. The argument against erecting a high fence or some other type of barrier has included the cost of construction, aesthetic concerns, and the belief that people who are thus prevented from jumping off the bridge will just find another way to kill themselves.

The barrier debate is not specific to the Golden Gate Bridge. As reported by Richard Bernstein in the *New York Times* on November 5, 1994, at Cornell University, where five separate bridges cross that campus's famous gorges, a local police officer proposed installing barriers to prevent "some suicides." Various arguments were made against the barriers, including one from the executive director of the local suicide-prevention center, who said that even if barriers were installed, people could "just go somewhere else." Despite this argument, suicidologists have maintained that "suicidal people are apt to choose a highly personal method, and if that method is unavailable they may abandon their plans rather than switch to another." (Colt, p. 333)

CHAPTER 7

COPING WITH THE SUICIDE OF SOMEONE YOU KNOW*

How do people react to the suicide of someone close to them? Is a loved one's suicide different from the death of a loved one from natural causes?

* This chapter does not cover coping with the aftermath of an assisted suicide. For information on that topic, please see chapter 8, "Assisted Suicide."

The sudden death of a loved one, whatever the cause, sets the survivor on a grief-stricken journey that in time ideally leads to an acceptance of the loss. A death by suicide can fill that journey with painful extra doses of shock, denial, guilt, blame, shame, anger, and a variety of other devastating and confusing emotions. In the pages that follow I discuss the feelings likely to be experienced by those left behind.

SHOCK

Twenty-five years later I can still picture and feel the moment in which I learned that my father was dead. Pills. It was a crushing, primal agony unlike anything I had ever known or have experienced since. When my mother broke the news to me, I yelled, "No!" and ran from her bedroom and locked myself in the bathroom—the only place where locked privacy was possible in our small apartment. I grabbed on to the towels hanging from the back of the bathroom door and pulled them down as I collapsed in a heap on the floor. I buried my head in the mound of cotton and screamed and screamed and screamed. At some point my twelve-year-old brain decided it needed to protect itself from the horror of what I'd just learned, and it turned itself off. I remember almost nothing about the rest of that day.

For me the immediate period after my father's death was characterized by a sense of unreality. I felt numb. I was dazed. I hardly cried. I remember everything that followed—from the funeral to the burial to going to synagogue every morning for a week to say the prayer for the dead—through a haze. I was disoriented. I couldn't sleep. I could hardly eat. I now know that what I experienced was shock and that what I felt is not at all uncommon for those who experience the sudden loss of a loved one through suicide.

DENIAL

My friend Don called one day from New Mexico about ten years ago to tell me that his mother was dead. She'd had a car accident. Drove her convertible right under the middle of a tractor trailer that was crossing an intersection in front of her. It was an accident, he insisted, denying what he and I both knew to be the truth. It was no accident. His mother had been depressed for as long as he could remember. Years before, we'd talked about his fear that she might one day take her life. But in the immediate aftermath of her death, there was no way he could simultaneously face the loss of his mother and the reality of her suicide. The loss was enough. He would deal with the suicide later, years later, once the initial grief had passed.

Confronted with the suicide of a loved one, some people refuse to accept what has happened. The pain of their loved one's choice is too much to comprehend, and denial kicks in. "No, it wasn't suicide." "It couldn't be." "It's a mistake." They convince themselves it was an accident that their mother drove under a truck, that their son overdosed on sleeping pills, or that their father jumped from an office building. Accidents. "She must have fallen asleep at the wheel." "He must have forgotten how many pills he'd taken." "He fell out the window." No matter how obvious the facts are to someone on the outside, people who are in denial can convince themselves of anything.

Denial can last a moment, as it did for me when I screamed "No!" It can last for days, or at least until a medical examiner confirms the awful truth. Or it can last for years or forever—no matter what anyone says, no matter what is demonstrated to the contrary. There is no getting around the fact of a loved one's death, but there is no end to the possibilities when it comes to ways in which you can convince yourself that the death occurred from natural causes.

In addition to standard denial, which I've just described, there's also something I call *official denial*. That's when the doctor and/or medical authorities conspire with family members to hide the truth. This is done, as it was in my father's case, with the best of intentions. To protect the family. To spare everyone the shame of a suicide and the judgment and/or condemnation of society. To keep the secret—which, unfortunately, also means never really dealing with and getting past the truth of what happened.

With my father it was easy to achieve official denial. By the time he died, four days after he'd overdosed on Librium, there wasn't a trace of the drug in his body. Official cause of death: pneumonia. I always got a chuckle out of that explanation. A man who was as strong as an ox, who days before was loading sacks of mail onto trucks, who just a week before was playing football with me, who was rarely if ever sick with even a cold (and who'd suffered for years from mental illness), died of natural causes. If the doctors or my family members thought anyone really believed that story, they were in serious denial. And, in fact, they were.

Even at twelve, I thought the whole thing was such a charade that I couldn't bear to tell anyone the official truth. I didn't think I could be convincing. But I didn't want to tell the *real* truth, either, because, judging from what everyone wasn't saying, I was convinced that suicide was so awful it was unutterable. So I generally avoided telling anyone that my father was dead. I just denied that anything had happened. When it came to denial in my family, I won hands down.

GRIEF

Intense grief is a perfectly normal reaction to the loss of a loved one. For someone who has lost that loved one to suicide, the grief may be even more intense and longer lasting. And for some people, the grief experience can be very physical. They lack energy, have trouble sleeping and eating, and may develop headaches and stomach problems.

Daniel was so overwhelmed by the grief he experienced over his older brother's suicide that he turned to drugs to kill the pain. When I spoke with him, it had been just a half year since his brother's death at age thirty. "We were best buddies from just about the day I was born," Daniel told me. "He was three years older than I am, and we did everything together. At first, I was just numb, bumping into walls. The first night, I fell asleep crying and I woke up crying hard. I cried so much that my vision was blurry."

During the first seven days following Daniel's brother's suicide, a period that included arranging and attending the funeral and visiting the house where his brother shot himself, Daniel was overwhelmed with grief. "It was so painful that I couldn't imagine how I'd get through it. So I bought a ton of dope, and whenever I was on the verge of feeling pain or crying, I'd smoke some. I've pretty much done that on and off since then, but I've quit for a while so I can start dealing with my emotions."

Daniel thought he was past the worst of his feelings of grief, but while reading the newspaper on the morning of the day we spoke, he came across the brand name of the gun his brother used, and it all came rushing back. "It was just one word that triggered it, that brought it all back. The feelings were as intense as as they were on day six or day seven, and it's a half year later. How much longer do I have to do this? I feel like I didn't get a good deal in life. I want my money back. It's six months and a day, and I want to get going."

Despite his frustration, Daniel knows that it will be a while longer—months, or perhaps years—before he is finished grieving the loss of his brother. "I know it will take me even longer if I keep doing dope," he said, "but there are times I just can't take the pain. I wish I were stronger."

Not everyone grieves the loss of a loved one right away. For children, especially, grieving may be unconsciously set aside. That was my experience. After the initial shock of my father's death, I went on with life, almost as if nothing had happened. Nearly a decade later I found myself in such a state of despair that I sought professional help and began seeing a psychologist once a week. Much to my surprise, I found myself propelled back into the painful period of my life following my father's death and began grieving his death for the first time.

REJECTION AND ABANDONMENT

The suicide of a loved one is the ultimate rejection. The person has gone forever, and those left behind, whether parents, children, spouses, or friends, can't help but feel rejected and/or abandoned.

ANGER

I think I'm still angry. I'm not as angry as I used to be, but as I write about this I'm aware that I am not writing dispassionately. Following is a list of some of the things that I was—and sometimes still am—angry about. I was/am angry at:

○ The Veterans Administration hospital where my father was treated, for not properly diagnosing his depression and for supplying him with the pills he used to kill himself. His suicide was paid for by the federal government.

○ My uncle and grandparents, for not having my father committed when they knew he was suicidal.

○ My mother, for not recognizing that my brother, sister, and I all needed counseling.

○ My father, for choosing to kill himself, for abandoning me, for destroying my family, for ruining my childhood, for leaving me with the legacy of suicide, for not giving me a chance to say good-bye.

○ My entire family, for pretending that my father didn't commit suicide and for making me feel ashamed of the truth.

Other people direct their anger at God or the mental-health authorities. They may also be angry at their dead loved one for:

○ Leaving them with unanswered questions.
○ Not giving them a chance to help.
○ Making them feel guilty.
○ Making them feel responsible for the suicide.
○ Making them feel ashamed and embarrassed.
○ Doing such a selfish thing.
○ Leaving them behind to deal with the police, the medical examiner, the morgue, the funeral home, the mess—both physical and emotional.

If their relationship with the person who committed suicide was a troubled one, those left behind may also be angry at him or her for robbing them of the chance to reconcile. Or they may be angry at themselves for not recognizing that there was a problem. They may even be angry at themselves for being angry.

Not everyone faced with a suicide experiences anger. In an interview in *Entertainment Weekly*, Wendy O'Connor, the mother of Kurt Cobain, the rock musician who killed himself in 1994, said, "People have asked me, aren't you angry at Kurt for taking such a cheap way out, for leaving Frances [his daughter] and you, and I said, no, not at all. People don't understand what depression is. . . . He was a wonderful person, but he just couldn't stand the pain anymore. That's why I'm not angry at Kurt."

GUILT

The primary reason people feel guilty is because they weren't able to do anything to prevent the suicide. They didn't get home in time, they had a fight with their loved one just before the suicide, they were too strict, they were too lenient, they weren't loving enough, they didn't get the right help, they failed to recognize that there was a problem, or they wished their loved one dead and told him or her so. The sense of guilt can be crushing, and it can last a lifetime.

I'm lucky, because I knew I wasn't responsible for my father's suicide, so I didn't feel guilty about that. I also knew that given my age and place in the family, I could not have been responsible for what he did, nor could I have done anything to prevent it.

Nonetheless, there was plenty for me to feel guilty about, just as there is for most people who live through a suicide. For example, I felt guilty for feeling relieved that my father was dead. (More on that later in this chapter.) I felt guilty for being angry at my father for committing suicide: he was dead; how could I be angry at him? And I feel guilty for having been angry at my father's brother for not doing more to prevent my father from killing himself: given how much my uncle has suffered over the years because of his own guilt, how could I be angry at him? Besides, it was my father who killed himself, and I'm not sure there was anything anyone could have done to prevent it. (I wish I could be 100 percent sure.)

Perhaps the worst guilt is that experienced by people who have unwittingly provided the means for the suicide. For example, the person who lends a gun to a trusted friend for an alleged hunting trip or the one who provides medical information and/or medication not knowing that it's going to be used for a suicide is likely to feel enormous guilt and responsibility.

BLAME

"For a long time, I blamed the psychologists," Carolyn told me, explaining her feelings about the suicide of her seventeen-year-old son more than a decade ago. "He had drug problems, he was depressed, he was angry, we couldn't control him. So we sent him to all kinds of counselors, and not one of them ever told us he was suicidal. I know all about the patient-client confidentiality business, but someone should have warned us what to look out for."

Carolyn saved plenty of blame for herself: "I really tortured myself, thinking I should have known he was suicidal. But it was something I wasn't familiar with. I didn't know anything about suicide, so I couldn't have known what symptoms to watch for. It wasn't until I walked in on him with the gun at his head that I realized he was suicidal. I had only a split second to say, 'Please, don't!' before he pulled the trigger. It was too late to stop him."

Blame is very tempting. As the years passed following my father's suicide and I became more aware of the circumstances around his suicide, I began to place blame. It was my uncle's fault that my father killed himself; he should have done *something* to stop him. It was my grandfather's fault; he was always so critical of my father. My mother should never have asked him for a separation; my father moved out on my mother's request two years before he committed suicide. The doctors were negligent. They were all to blame.

For a long time, I never thought to blame my father for his own suicide. It was, after all, his choice, but I didn't think to blame him, and when those thoughts crept into mind, I felt guilty for thinking them and pushed them away. After all, my father was the victim of the neglect of others, of their failure to see what was going on, of their failure to intervene. If only they'd done the right thing, he'd still be alive. Wouldn't he?

I remember being shocked, right after Dad died, by my father's friend Howard. Howard called up one day shortly after the funeral. I answered the phone. He didn't want to talk to my mom, and it was clear to me that he was angry at her for my father's death. I instinctively knew that he blamed her. I was years away from thinking in terms of blame, so I found the whole thing confusing, especially since everyone else expressed sympathy over my father's death.

Howard, who was an artist, said he wanted to come by to pick up a painting he'd given to my father. This particular painting, which happened to be a favorite of mine, was of my father as a monk, sitting in the burned-out wreckage of an old wood house. Only the frame of the building still stood, and my father was looking up at the moon through the charred timbers with a bewildered look on his face. Even before Dad's suicide, I thought the visual metaphor fit. Now that my father was dead, I thought of that painting as mine. I told my mother what Howard wanted, and she said he could come by the next evening to pick it up. I was too young to argue with her over how I felt, and I didn't care to fight with Howard.

When Howard came by, I answered the door. He didn't want to see my mother, and he made that clear. He handed me a small football he'd brought with him, took the painting from the wall, and left. We never heard from him again. I've always wondered in what way Howard thought my father's death was my mother's doing. Maybe he never knew how intolerable life had been for my mother before my parents separated. I imagine he saw her decision to separate as the catalyst for Dad's suicide.

For years I was tempted to try to find Howard, in part to find out what had been going through his mind back then, but mostly because I wanted my painting back.

SELF-RECRIMINATION

"If only . . . " It's the start of a phrase that's thought and spoken by almost everyone who has felt responsible for not preventing the suicide of a loved one. "If only I'd come home earlier." "If only I'd known there was a problem." "If only I hadn't yelled at him." "If only I'd told her I loved her." "If only I'd been more understanding." "If only I'd dragged him to a psychiatrist."

Whenever my grandmother and I talk about my father's death, there's always one thing I can count on her to say: "If only I hadn't gone to Florida." When my father swallowed that ultimately fatal dose of pills, his parents were in Florida visiting with my grandmother's brother, who was seriously ill. My grandmother had been torn between staying home and keeping in close contact with my father, who had recently been hospitalized for depression, and seeing her brother. While she was away, her worst fear came true.

No matter what I say, and no matter how many times I say it, my grandmother can't help but blame herself, believing that if only she'd not gone away, my father would be alive today. There's no way to know exactly what would have happened if my grandmother hadn't gone to Florida, but I feel certain my father would have killed himself anyway—if not on that particular weekend, then another time. I wish my grandmother could believe that.

CONFUSION

The suicide of a loved one leaves in its wake painful confusion that's expressed with a one-word question: *Why?* Embedded in that question are three others that begin with *why:* Why didn't we see it coming? Why didn't he/she come to us for help? And above all else, Why did he/she do it?

Daniel is still asking himself why his brother committed suicide. Daniel's brother had recently bought a new house following a painful separation from his wife. "He seemed real excited about the house and was getting it ready for his two kids to visit. It wasn't like he was unemployed or anything; he had a good job. I thought he had everything to live for. Sure, his wife was getting remarried to someone he didn't like, but that's no reason to blow your head off. I want to know why he did it. Why would he do this to his kids? To me? I have this sinking feeling that I'll never know the answer. I'm not even sure *he* knew why."

In their search for answers, Daniel and his parents went to the house where his brother committed suicide. "We took the place apart, trying to find a clue, a reason, an answer—something. But there was nothing, except for the bloodstained carpet in the room where he shot himself."

RELIEF

I am embarrassed to admit that one of the first things I felt once I got over the initial shock of my father's suicide was relief. Part of me thought his death was a good thing. I was certain that God—or someone—would punish me for feeling that way, so I never told anyone. But I had a couple of good reasons for feeling as I did.

The primary reason had to do with the relationship between my mom and dad. They had been through an extremely painful and stormy separation two years before my father committed suicide. The welcome calm that settled over our once-tense household after Dad moved out was threatened by my father's clandestine visits to the apartment when my brother, sister, and I were at school and my mother was at work.

In the weeks before my father's death, my mother talked about changing the locks on the door to our apartment. I was terrified of the confrontation that I knew would follow. Dad's death meant that the confrontation would never take place. How could I not have been relieved?

There was another reason I was relieved. Because my dad had emotional problems, I feared he'd wind up institutionalized. I imagined how terrible it would be to visit him after he was locked up in a state mental hospital; my twelve-year-old imagination conjured up a Dickensian image. I also didn't know how I'd explain to friends that my dad was in a mental hospital. His death meant I'd never have to deal with that, either.

Feeling relieved following the suicide of a loved one is not uncommon. I take comfort in that fact, and it makes me feel less guilty. Feeling relieved is likely when the person who committed suicide was in some way a burden in life. For example, if a loved one had struggled with chronic depression or schizophrenia, had been in and out of hospitals, or had been abusing drugs and/or alcohol, his or her death is likely to be something of a relief. There may also be a sense of relief when the person who committed suicide had been suffering from physical infirmity caused by illness and/or old age.

Relief is a troubling emotion in the context of the suicide of a loved one. But whether we're at peace with that feeling or experience tremendous guilt, there's no getting around the fact that sometimes there are moments when people feel relieved that their loved one is dead.

COMPASSION

When Leslie's sixty-three-year-old father took his life, what she experienced most strongly was a sense of compassion. Leslie's father had been depressed all his life, and no treatment seemed to help him out of his despair. Leslie told me: "Nothing worked, and he tried everything, from shock treatment to the latest antidepressants. You can't imagine how many doctors he went to see and how frustrating it was for him. He really suffered."

Leslie always thought her father would wind up killing himself. Still, it was a shock. "No matter how much you prepare for something like that, it always comes as a surprise. But I wasn't angry. How could I be? He was in pain, and he'd had enough. I think it would be selfish of me to feel angry or abandoned or any of those things people usually feel. I was sad, but more than anything, I felt compassion for a man who I loved and who I'd watched suffer for as long as I can remember. He's at peace now. And I don't care what other people think, because other people don't know how hellish his life was."

SHAME AND EMBARRASSMENT

From the way my family dealt with the nature of my father's death, it was clear to me that they were embarrassed over what he did and that they felt that what he did was shameful. Why else all the whispers, the closed doors, and the invented cause of death?

The shame and embarrassment people experience over suicide is complex. Some of it has to do with how Western society viewed suicide in centuries past—when suicide was considered a criminal offense and the surviving relatives were punished for the suicide of a family member. And it wasn't just the families that were punished. The person who committed suicide was forbidden a proper burial because taking one's life was considered sinful.

Today we no longer punish the families of suicide victims, suicide is generally not considered sinful by mainstream religions, and suicide victims are buried in cemeteries like everyone else. Yet plenty of people still make hurtful judgments about those who commit suicide and look down on the family members they leave behind. The person who committed suicide is seen as defective, the parents as incompetent, and the spouse as awful. How, people ask, could a suicide happen in a good family? There must be something wrong with the family.

Of course, it isn't only people from the outside looking in who make these judgments. Those of us who have lived through the suicide of a loved one make those judgments about ourselves, which leads many of us to feel ashamed and embarrassed, and highly motivated to keep the suicide a family secret. Unfortunately, keeping this secret leaves us feeling alone and isolated.

ISOLATION

Many people who live through the suicide of a loved one feel all alone in the world, as if they're the only ones who have had this experience. Part of the reason they feel this way is because they're too embarrassed, ashamed, grief-stricken, and/or guilt-ridden over the suicide to share their story with anyone. Or they simply don't know anyone who has had a similar experience.

It doesn't help much to know that thousands and thousands of people every year experience the suicide of a loved one. Those are just numbers. Unless you actually talk to someone who has been through the same thing, it's easy to feel entirely alone, as if no one has any idea of what you're going through.

DEPRESSION

Given how traumatic a suicide is and how difficult it can be to cope with the emotional turmoil that follows, it's not surprising that people who lose a loved one to suicide may become depressed. Feelings of depression are normal and become a problem only when they persist and/or become incapacitating.

SUICIDAL FEELINGS

I think about suicide a lot, and not just because I wrote this book. From an early age, I wondered if I would wind up just like my father. Would life ever become so intolerable that I, too, would want to take my life? Then once I learned that I was at greater risk for suicide because my father killed himself, I really started to worry that I was destined to follow in his footsteps.

Some people who experience the suicide of a loved one have thoughts of suicide in the immediate aftermath. Their thoughts have to do with a desire to end the pain of their grief and/or a desire to be reunited with their loved one.

For others, like me, these feelings are the result of suicide being introduced as an option. In other words, if your parent, sibling, or friend could do this, then you can, too. As time has passed, I've grown less uncomfortable with, and less frightened of, my thoughts about suicide. I know these are thoughts that many people have, especially those who have lived through the suicide of a parent. I also know that despite the fact that I'm at greater risk because of what my father did, I'm not compelled to act on my suicidal feelings.

FEAR

Besides fearing for oneself because of suicidal feelings, as I did, people are bound to worry about other family members committing suicide once a parent, sibling, child, or friend has done it.

After Carolyn's son killed himself, one of the things she feared most was that one of her other children might commit suicide. "I had no reason to believe that any of them was suicidal, but then I never thought my son would kill himself. So I watched my other children like a hawk. If they were suicidal I didn't want to miss any clues. I know I made them crazy with the way I worried and questioned them, but for the first couple of years, I couldn't help it."

For other people, their fear has nothing to do with the living. They are fearful that their dead loved one will not go to heaven because he or she committed suicide. I like to think that of the many reasons people don't go to heaven, suicide is not among them.

○ *What is the impact on families? How do families react?*

Just as a suicide can devastate individuals, its impact on a family—the complex web that includes brothers, sisters, parents, friends, uncles, aunts, and cousins—can be monumental. Some families are blown apart by the guilt and blame that can follow a suicide. Some are drawn together, rallying to support one another as they struggle through their individual and collective grief and confusion. Other families continue on in silence, pretending as best they can that nothing has happened or that the suicide was an accidental death.

In the case of my own family, my father's suicide blew apart already strained and fragile familial ties. My family has never recovered. I think of my father's suicide as an emotional bomb that he set off in our living room. No one was killed, but people were scattered in all directions and the emotional wreckage was everywhere.

In the immediate aftermath, my older sister, who was seventeen, retreated emotionally and physically from the family. My favorite (and only) uncle, my father's brother, virtually disappeared, despite the fact that he lived a half hour away. My father's closest friends, who were made to feel unwelcome, faded from our lives. My father's parents struggled to go on as if nothing had happened, believing they could best help their loved ones by sparing us the grief that threatened to engulf them. My mother was a blur, busy supporting three children and struggling with her own emotional turmoil. My younger brother and I shared the same tiny bedroom but lived in virtual isolation from each other. It wasn't until years after I'd left home that my brother and I talked about the nature of our father's death for the first time. We have hardly spoken of it since.

Shattered, scattered, angry, bereft, bewildered, guilt-ridden, ashamed, we all went about nursing our wounds in different ways, some of us eventually struggling to come to terms with it on our own, reaching out painfully on occasion through the years to share the struggle, but never as a family.

My father killed himself and in doing so just about killed our family, but fortunately that is not everyone's experience. In contrast, the death of Daniel's brother brought together a badly fractured family. Daniel's parents, who were both divorced and remarried, had for years communicated only through their children. Daniel and his mother hadn't talked in two years about the fact that he was gay. "She wanted nothing to do with me. So when I got the news from my father that my brother had committed suicide, I didn't exactly volunteer to call her."

Daniel's father offered him the choice of calling his other brother or his mother. Daniel was even more estranged from his brother, so he agreed to call his mother. His friend Joan held his hand while he made the call. "I hung up the first time because I didn't know what to do. I told my mom to sit down, to take a deep breath. I told her point-blank that my brother had killed himself. She screamed and I told her I'd call her back. I let three minutes pass and called again to tell her that I'd pick her up at the airport that night."

Daniel was very anxious and nervous as he drove to the airport, but seeing his mother again wasn't as bad as he had anticipated. "Given what had just happened, I think it was of some comfort for both of us to see each other again, and there was so much to arrange that we didn't have much of a chance to focus on the fact we hadn't talked to each other in two years."

In the six months since the suicide, Daniel's mother has been to visit twice, and they speak frequently by phone. "She now accepts that she has a gay son, and we've started sharing things. She'll call up just to talk about what happened during the day or to talk about my brother and how she's feeling about it. And I call her." Daniel also has more contact with both his father and brother. "I'm more likely to tell my father what I think now, and we talk about what happened to my brother. My other brother, who never called me in the past, calls up and just bursts into tears. He's having a real hard time with this, and it turns out that I'm the one he feels most comfortable talking to."

Almost everyone in Daniel's family has sought some kind of professional counseling, and they've even talked about going to counseling together as a family. "We've talked about it, but there's so much other stuff that we haven't dealt with as a family that we're all a little reluctant. I know it would do a lot of good, but we're not there yet."

○ *How do husbands/wives react to the suicide of a spouse?*

How a surviving husband or wife reacts depends a lot on the condition of the marriage and the circumstances of the suicide. But most often, a surviving spouse feels guilty for not having prevented the suicide, as well as rejected and/or abandoned. Even if their relationship was a good one, the suicide is likely to be interpreted as something of a referendum on their married life. The surviving spouse may also feel shame, fearing that others will look on him or her as having been so awful to live with that the spouse was driven to suicide.

For Michael, his wife's suicide on her birthday sent a message, whether or not it was intended. "She didn't leave a note, but one of our running arguments had been that I never remembered her birthday. I can't imagine it was a coincidence that she shot herself on that day and that she chose our bedroom as the place to do it. We had problems like everyone else, but I didn't think they were anything out of the ordinary. Apparently she did."

Relationship problems weren't the only thing Michael's wife had on her mind at the time she killed herself. Michael explained that his wife had recently been fired from her job as an office manager because of a drinking problem. "They warned her. I begged her to get help. But she didn't think she had a problem. The drinking apparently contributed to the suicide, because she was quite drunk when she shot herself. So if I can take any comfort in this, it's that she wasn't thinking clearly when she did it."

Alison's husband, Allen, was also under the influence of alcohol when he drowned himself in the swimming pool of his apartment complex. "He'd also swallowed a bottle of liquid antihistamine and a bottle of Tylenol tablets. Apparently they didn't work fast enough, and after filling three legal pads with his thoughts, he threw himself into the pool." But unlike Michael, Alison didn't feel rejected or that her husband's suicide was in any way a comment on their marriage. "He was a very depressed young man when I met him, and I guess I figured I could save him. I couldn't."

After five years of marriage, Alison and Allen decided it would be best to separate. During the time they were married, Allen had been unable to work, and Alison was the primary wage earner. Allen spent much of his time caring for their daughter, Rachel, who was born a year after he and Alison were married.

The breaking point for Allen came on the day he and Alison were supposed to sign formal separation papers. "He completely wigged out. That night he came over to the house and apologized for all the horrible things he'd said to me earlier in the day and told me what a wonderful mother I was and how proud he was of Rachel. It sounded to me like he was giving a farewell speech, but I put that out of my head. I didn't want to think about it."

As Allen was leaving Alison's house to go back to his apartment, he asked her if he could spend the night. "I told him I didn't think it was a good idea, and he left. The next morning I went to work and his mother called me to ask if I knew where he was. My heart dropped. I think in that moment I knew he'd done something crazy. I got in my car and drove to his apartment. The police were already there. They'd just pulled him out of the pool and he was lying on the deck. I became hysterical—just to see him there completely lifeless. I felt guilt, tremendous guilt. I believe I did the right thing by not letting him stay over that night, but it's been several years since his death and I still feel a twinge of guilt that I was responsible—even though I know I wasn't."

It was only recently that Alison started feeling that her late husband had abandoned her. "Now that Rachel is getting older and is involved in various activities at school, it's hard for me being the only parent. It makes me angry. And it also makes me angry that he's left such a burden for Rachel. This is something she's going to have to deal with for the rest of her life."

How do parents react?

Parents are left wondering what they did wrong. Were they too strict? Were they not strict enough? Were they too attentive? Were they not attentive enough? Even parents of children who are well into adulthood are left wondering, "Was I a bad parent?"

When my grandmother and I talked about my father's suicide, she reviewed my father's childhood, recalling disagreements between mother and son that she thought might have led to the emotional problems that eventually caused a forty-four-year-old man to commit suicide. How could she not wonder? How could she not feel that his death was a reflection on her abilities as a mother? It seems the most natural thing in the world for a parent to do, even if there are no real answers.

For parents, the suicide of a child also brings extra doses of guilt and self-recrimination. A parent is supposed to know and protect his or her child. How could a parent let that happen? And as if the self-recrimination weren't enough, there are the fears about how others will view them as parents. What must people think of them? What terrible things do people think they did that led their child to kill himself or herself?

○ *How does the suicide of a child affect the ability of parents*
   to be good parents to their surviving children?

Parents who have lost one child to suicide may react to their
other children in a number of different and conflicting ways
that can make it difficult to be good parents. They may become fearful that their other children will commit suicide or
that something will happen to them, and so become overly
protective. Or their confidence in their abilities to parent may
be so shaken that they're unable to be as strong and supportive
as their children need them to be in a time of crisis. They may
also be so absorbed in their own grief that they withdraw from
their children, becoming neglectful just when their children
need them most.

Parents who are incapacitated by grief may also find themselves swapping roles with their surviving children. The children take on the role of parent, offering comfort, taking care
of funeral and other necessary arrangements following the suicide, and managing everyday tasks until the grieving parents
are back on their feet.

○ *How do couples react to the suicide of a child?*

It is not uncommon for marriages to be strained to the breaking point over the suicide of a child. The grief, guilt, and
blame quickly tear at the fibers that hold a marriage together.
Some couples are ultimately destroyed by the experience, others weather it, supporting each other through the ordeal, and
still others retreat into silence, enduring the pain of their loss
in isolation.

For Carolyn, whose seventeen-year-old son shot himself at
home, the suicide was almost the end of her thirty-three-year

marriage. She told me: "Our marriage barely survived it. The reason the marriage ultimately survived was that I read every book on grief. I went to a counselor. I had to make it survive. My husband did not read. He did not talk. He kept everything inside."

Shortly after the suicide, Carolyn's husband began to drink heavily. "He couldn't deal with the pain. I told him a month or two after he began drinking, 'I understand why you're drinking, but I have to tell you I can't handle my grief and your drinking at the same time. Either you quit or we'll have to separate.' And he quit. I know he did his work in his own way, but he couldn't verbalize anything."

Over the years, I wondered how my grandparents dealt with my father's suicide. Despite the difficulties they had with my father because of his radical politics and severe depressions, he was still their first and much-loved son. I asked my grandmother about this recently, and she said that in the two decades between my father's suicide and my grandfather's death, she and my grandfather never talked about it. I know I must have had a shocked look on my face, and my grandmother elaborated, explaining that they talked about my father, but that each respected the other's feelings and never raised the subject of his suicide.

○ *How do young children react to the suicide of a parent?*

I used to be proud of the way I reacted to my father's suicide. After the initial shock wore off, I went back to my life as if nothing had happened. I missed only one day of school. I didn't have outbursts or cry uncontrollably. I was stoic and mature about the whole thing. As several of my relatives reminded me at the funeral, I was the man of the family now. I took my job seriously.

There were only a couple of clues that there was anything really wrong, and it wasn't until years later that I figured this out. I had always done well in school, but in the months after my father died I had trouble with some of my classes and almost failed a couple of them. Also, within a few months of my dad's death I developed a skin disorder that required weekly visits to the dermatologist for years.

I know now that I did what a lot of kids do when faced with the death of a parent—whether or not it's from suicide. The whole experience was so overwhelming that I put off grieving until I was older and capable of handling it. This was not something I consciously did (other than making an effort to "be a man" about the whole thing). My defense mechanisms did it for me. When I finally sought the help of a psychologist in my early twenties, it was because I was depressed and concerned about my suicidal thoughts. I didn't know it had anything to do with my father's death until I started talking.

Kids who have been through the suicide of a parent can experience a whole range of emotions and express them in different ways. They may feel rejected by the parent who has committed suicide. They may blame the surviving parent for causing the suicide. Or they may blame themselves, thinking that if they had been a better child, then Mommy or Daddy wouldn't have chosen to leave. If they had ever secretly wished that parent dead, they'll likely feel guilty for having somehow caused the death by the very act of wishing. They may also feel that they were so bad that the parent chose to leave. They may cling to the surviving parent, fearing the loss of that parent, too. Or they may cling to a favorite doll or pet. (My cat Tiger was a tremendous comfort to me.)

Some children begin to have problems with nightmares. Others withdraw from their friends, spending increasing amounts of time alone. They may also act out in all kinds of ways, from cutting classes and failing at school to taking drugs. Other kids react in quite the opposite way and become hyperresponsible, taking care of their grieving mother or father in the immediate aftermath of the suicide.

For Alison's daughter, Rachel, the problems were more with other people's reactions to how Rachel dealt with her father's suicide than with how she herself dealt with it. "Rachel was only four, but she seemed to accept pretty well what happened. She seemed sad, but other than that, she really was herself. I feel awkward saying it, but I feel lucky that my husband killed himself when he did. If Rachel had been older I think she would have taken the loss much harder and she would have also had an understanding of the stigma of suicide. I also think that what helped her was my honesty about the whole thing. She knew from the very beginning exactly what happened to her father."

The first hint of trouble came when Alison got a telephone call from Rachel's kindergarten teacher. "She called to tell me that the other children were getting scared when Rachel said her father committed suicide. And that got the kids started asking the teacher questions about suicide and she didn't know what to say. I told her she'd have to deal with it, because I didn't want Rachel to feel there was any reason to hide the truth."

No matter how a child reacts to the suicide of a mother or father, keep in mind that to a child the loss of a parent is enormously traumatic no matter what the cause of death. When that death is a suicide, when that parent has actively chosen to leave, the impact is even greater. And as the child grows up, he or she will have to wrestle with what his or her parent has done. Was this the right choice? Is suicide a viable alternative? It's a hell of a legacy.

Following the suicide of a parent, children need consistent love and support, which is exactly what Alison gave to Rachel. Ironically, the immediate aftermath of a suicide is just the time when a child is likely to be ignored by the surviving parent and the other adults in that child's life. Often these people are so preoccupied with their own grief that they overlook the needs of the child. Or they may assume that the child is not affected in the same way they are and therefore doesn't need special attention.

Children are not likely to react in the same way adults do. They may not do anything more than shed a few tears and remain quiet. But don't let that fool you: often they are acutely aware of everything that has happened.

Is the suicide of a parent different for adult children?

No matter how awful it is to have a parent commit suicide, the experience of an adult whose parent commits suicide is fundamentally different from that of a young child. Besides having both a level of understanding and coping skills that children don't, grown children are not wholly dependent upon their parents in the way young children are. So whereas adult children are likely to be devastated, their day-to-day home life is not shattered by the sudden absence of a parent who has committed suicide. And though their sense of loss and abandonment in the aftermath of the suicide may be profound, it is likely to pale in comparison to what is experienced by a child.

Not every adult child is devastated or left bewildered by the suicide of a parent. A year ago, Evelyn's eighty-five-year-old father committed suicide by locking himself in his garage and turning on his car. "It was a real blow, especially since my mother had died just a few months before, but I was more sad than anything. It was clear to me that Father was simply at sea without my mother. He'd said a number of times how he didn't want to go on without her, but I didn't take that to mean he would kill himself. It seemed perfectly rational for him to say that he didn't want to go on without her. I guess I feel more than a little guilty, too, because I didn't listen clearly to what he was saying."

○ *How do you explain a suicide to a child?*

Whether the person who has committed suicide is a parent, sibling, grandparent, close family friend, or some other important person in a child's life, the parents (or surviving parent) need to tell the truth about what has happened. This doesn't mean explaining the suicide in the kind of detail you might use when talking to a close adult friend, but it does mean explaining what happened in clear terms a child can understand. And it means being prepared to answer in a direct way the questions that will inevitably follow.

If you're thinking of hiding the truth from your child, you need to consider a number of things. First, even if you haven't said anything, your child may already know the truth. That was my experience, and I know I'm not alone.

No one told me that my father committed suicide. I overheard my mother's conversation with my aunt the day my father was found. From what my mother said in response to my aunt, I learned that my father was in the hospital. Then after a long pause, I heard my mother say the word *pills* in a way that made it clear she was repeating something my aunt had said to her. I had no trouble drawing my own conclusions.

When my father died several days later, the official word was that he had died of pneumonia. What that lie indicated to me was that suicide was a terrible and embarrassing thing. My father's death was something to be ashamed of. I also learned that adults weren't to be trusted: they lie. I know these weren't the messages my family wanted to convey to me, but that's what I received.

Kids take the lead from the adults around them. If you indicate by your actions that suicide is something so awful and shameful that you have to lie about it, your child will respond accordingly, and you will rob him or her of the chance to deal with the loss in a constructive way. If, on the other hand, you are direct, honest, and supportive, you will help your child begin to heal.

Knowing what I know now about suicide, and given my experience, this is how I wish my mother had explained things to me (and ideally, she would have been supported in this by my father's family):

"Your father loved you very much, but you know that he was very unhappy and that he had emotional problems. [My father's emotional problems were no secret to me; I got to observe his depressions and bouts of paranoia firsthand.] The pain had become so great for him that he decided he couldn't go on any longer. He swallowed a lot of pills. The doctors tried everything they could at the hospital, but there was nothing they could do."

I would have wanted to know a lot more, but these simple sentences would have been all the opening I needed to ask the other things I wanted to know, from whether my father had left a note (he did, but I didn't learn about it until ten years later) to why the doctors couldn't save him. Ideally, I would have been able to ask anything, with no question off limits. But without that opening, there was no way for me to ask anything. And from the way the adults were acting, I knew that I shouldn't.

When Alison's husband, Allen, drowned himself, there was never any doubt in Alison's mind that she was going to tell her daughter the truth. "After they took away Allen's body, all I could think about was getting Rachel out of school before word filtered out that Allen had killed himself. I wanted to get her home and keep her safe. I wanted to talk to her and tell her what happened before anyone else did. I wanted her to know from the very beginning that he took his own life. I didn't want her to have to learn about this years later and then find myself having to explain why I'd kept it secret from her."

Once they got home, Alison sat Rachel down and started explaining. "She was only four, so I told her that some people's bodies get sick and they die and some people's minds get sick and they die. I explained to her that her father's mind was sick and that it wasn't his fault. I said, 'He was very sad, and he took some drugs and drowned himself.'" Rachel listened carefully to her mother, her eyes filled with tears. When her mother was finished, Rachel said simply, "I just wish I could have said good-bye."

Rachel didn't have a lot of questions initially, but over the years she's come to her mother on many occasions to ask questions. "She knows that she can ask me anything anytime and that I'll give a straight answer. I'm grateful for that—that she feels she can ask me anything."

If you're not sure what approach to take with your child, get advice from an expert. You have a tremendous responsibility to help your child through this experience, and what you do and say can have an enormous positive—or negative—impact. Talk to a social worker at the hospital where your spouse or loved one died. Call a suicide hot line. However you do it, get the help you need to help your child (or children) as best you can.

○ *How do people react to the suicide of a sibling?*

A lot depends on the age of the surviving siblings, their stage in life, and the nature of their relationship with the person who committed suicide. For example, my uncle's experience of my father's suicide was intensified by the fact that my father, his brother, was twelve years older and was more of a father to my uncle than a brother. From just about the day my uncle was born, my father took him everywhere with him. My father was his best buddy, his teacher, and someone he could always count on to protect him. So, added to the crushing blow of losing a brother who had been like a father to him was the overwhelming guilt my uncle felt because he had failed to save the brother who had protected him from harm.

Although adult siblings have many different kinds of complex reactions to the suicide of a brother or sister, the siblings who are affected most profoundly and predictably are generally those who are still living at home. Jennifer was sixteen when her twenty-one-year-old sister took an overdose of pills while she was away at college. That was ten years ago. "Everything changed," she told me. "My parents were so caught up in Cindy's death that they seemed to forget that I was alive. I began to wonder if maybe I'd get more attention if I were dead."

In retrospect, Jennifer now realizes that she deliberately started getting in trouble at school to get attention from her parents. "I didn't know how else to let them know I needed them. It was a good thing that my idea of trouble was staying out past my curfew and failing a couple of tests. My parents were so oblivious that I could have really gotten in a lot of trouble if I'd been more fearless. Looking back, it seems so obvious that I was suffering, too. Cindy was my sister, and we shared a room until I was thirteen years old. Her death was horrible for me, too, but my parents were so destroyed they couldn't see beyond their own suffering for more than a year."

In contrast to Jennifer's experience, surviving siblings sometimes find themselves the focus of intense parental attention because the parents fear that their other children will follow the lead of the dead sibling. In that case the surviving siblings may rebel against parents who are suddenly overly protective.

Like other siblings who have lost a sister or brother to suicide, Jennifer found that despite her grief over Cindy's death, she felt resentful toward her dead sister. "That made me feel even worse. But she ruined everything. I genuinely had a happy home life. We all got along. I loved my parents, and my parents loved me and Cindy both. That's what made the whole thing so shattering. And it was all her fault, or at least that's how I felt when I was at my worst."

Surviving siblings also sometimes find themselves switching roles with their parents, as Daniel did, and wind up being parents to their own parents while they struggle through their grief.

○ *How do people react to the suicide of a teenager or young person?*

In addition to the expected reactions to any suicide, people feel particularly bewildered by the suicide of a teenager or young person. How, we ask, could someone with so much life to look forward to end it before it's really started? This is especially true when we hear of the suicide of a star student at a prestigious college or university.

Besides the terrible impact on the immediate family and loved ones, there is the effect on other parents, who can't help but wonder, "Could this happen in my family?" Young friends ask themselves, "Could this happen to me? Is that the answer to my problems?" And both friends and teachers are left wondering, "Is there something I could have done to prevent it?"

○ *How do people react to someone who has lost a loved one to suicide?*

People react in a variety of ways, depending on the circumstances. But in general, reactions range from compassion and understanding to extreme discomfort and awkwardness.

HOW PEOPLE REACT CONSTRUCTIVELY

- ○ They reach out in some manner to let the grief-stricken person know that they care and can be counted on for support.
- ○ They offer to go with him or her to a support group.
- ○ They volunteer to look after the children.

HOW PEOPLE REACT NEGATIVELY

- ○ They act awkward and distant.
- ○ They avoid the person who has lost a loved one to suicide.

○ They forbid their children to play with the children of a family in which someone has committed suicide.

○ They judge a person negatively because of the suicide of that person's spouse or child.

○ They condemn someone who has committed suicide for having been a coward or sinner.

Not all those who respond with silence or awkwardness are passing judgment. They may genuinely care, yet not say anything because they don't want to add to the upset or simply don't know what to say.

○ *What should you do when someone you know has lost a loved one to suicide? What should you say?*

When someone you know loses a loved one to suicide, you need to give him or her enough room to grieve, but not so much room that he or she feels abandoned or shunned. If you withdraw, whatever the reason, your absence will be noticed and not easily forgiven. However you do it—by phone, in a letter, or in person—you need to convey that you care and that it's okay to talk about it. For example, to a coworker you can say: "I heard the news. I'm so sorry. This must be terrible for you. How are you doing? I'm here if you need me."

Keep in mind that the person who is grieving will need even more support over a longer period of time than someone who has lost a loved one from natural causes. Compassion and understanding are key. It never hurts to ask, "How are you doing?"

Though there are no hard and fast rules about what you should say to someone dealing with the suicide of a loved one, there are definitely things you should avoid saying and asking.

WHAT NOT TO ASK
Didn't you see it coming?

Most likely, they already feel guilty for not having seen it coming and don't need anyone implying that they weren't paying attention.

Why?

There is almost never an adequate answer to the "why" question, and asking just accentuates that fact. Besides, they've probably been asking themselves that question a thousand times a day since the suicide, so why make it a thousand and one?

WHAT NOT TO SAY
It was God's will.

Even if they're religious, this is not likely to be any comfort and will probably be greeted with anger.

Suicide is sinful and your loved one will suffer in damnation.

If you sincerely believe this, keep it to yourself. Expressing this sentiment will only hurt your friend or loved one and drive him or her away.

At least she/he is out of pain.

When the person who commits suicide is someone who has suffered from lifelong depression, for example, you may be tempted to offer comfort to those left behind by looking on the bright side. This is not likely to be of any comfort to the bereaved and is best not shared.

It's time to get over it. You've been sad long enough.

You may have legitimate concerns that your friend or loved one has been grief-stricken longer than what one might expect. But saying it's time to "get over it" is not a constructive way of dealing with this concern. Consider encouraging your friend or loved one to see a counselor or join a support group. You can even track down the information yourself. Or consult a counselor to find out how you might be of help.

I know how you feel.

You can be terribly sorry. You can even know what it means to lose someone you love. But unless you've been through a suicide, you can't genuinely know what your friend or loved one is going through and what he or she is feeling. Though it may seem like an innocent thing to say, unless you've experienced the suicide of someone close to you, don't attempt to offer comfort by saying this.

However, if you do have firsthand experience with the loss of someone to suicide, by all means, share it. Your friend or loved one will appreciate talking to someone who understands completely what he or she is going through.

○ ○ ○

Above all, however uncomfortable you may feel about dealing with someone who has lost a loved one to suicide, don't pretend it didn't happen. Otherwise your friend or loved one will feel abandoned at a time when he or she needs you most.

○ *What is it like to find a loved one who has committed suicide?*

Traumatic. Shocking. Horrifying. No adjective quite describes the experience. For years, the image of her son shooting himself in the head was the last thing Carolyn saw at night before falling asleep and the first thing she saw in the morning. "It was like being battered by a wave on the shore. It was all I could see."

Carolyn's teenage daughter rushed to her brother's side as Carolyn frantically called for help. "If I'd been thinking, I never would have let her go into his room. He was convulsing and bleeding from his nose and mouth. I don't think she's ever recovered. It's been more than ten years, but she still won't talk about it with me or anyone."

Daniel was relieved that he wasn't the one to find his brother's body, but within days of the suicide he and his parents went to the house where the suicide took place. "We were advised by everyone not to go to the house, but my mother and her husband, and my father and his wife, and I went to the house to search for clues in the hopes we'd find something that would make his death more clear."

By the time Daniel's brother was found, he'd already been dead for two days. Another two days passed before the family searched the house. "I just remember that the house smelled horrible, and that I couldn't hear anything but the sound of blood rushing through my ears. We went through every room searching for clues and went into his bedroom last. When I saw the puddle of blood, I just wanted to get us all out of there, but it was too late. My parents just crumbled. Dad knelt down and touched the dried puddle of blood and started sobbing. Mom screamed and collapsed onto the bed. They were my parents. They were supposed to be the strong ones, but now I had to be the parent, and I told them this was too much and I escorted them out to the yard."

A little while later, Daniel went back to the bedroom. "I was more calm this time and I had a chance to look around. He must have shot himself downward because there was a bullet hole by the bottom of the window, and a splat. I cried for the rest of the day. Given how awful it was seeing the room where my brother shot himself, I think if I'd been the one to find him, I'd still be throwing up."

○ *What about having to identify the body?*

Having to identify the body can also be traumatic, especially when the suicide has been a violent one, as it was in the case of Daniel's brother. Daniel was going to identify his brother's body so his parents wouldn't have to, although it wasn't something he wanted to do. "At the last minute, one of my stepbrothers volunteered. It was a total relief. I can't imagine how awful it would have been to have that as my last memory of my brother."

In my family, my uncle, who was thirty-two at the time, was the one who identified my father's body. Until he and I talked recently about the details regarding my father's suicide, it hadn't even occurred to me that someone would have had to identify the body.

Because of the nature of my father's death, an autopsy was required, and following the autopsy, before the body could be released to the funeral home, someone had to identify it. My uncle's description of the horrifying scene at the morgue and the condition of my father's body called forth images I can't wash from my mind's eye. Nothing made me understand more clearly the trauma my uncle lived through than hearing his description of identifying his brother's body at the morgue. If I harbored any feelings of blame toward my uncle before that conversation, I had only compassion for him afterward.

I'm glad my uncle and I talked. For me, learning about the details of my father's suicide, its aftermath, and everyone's role has been important. But, regarding identifying the body at least, I'm almost sorry I asked.

○ *Are people at greater risk of suicide following the suicide of someone they know? Are children of people who commit suicide at special risk?*

There are statistics and studies showing that those who are left behind are at greater risk of suicide, especially the family members and children of someone who has committed suicide. I have known this for a long time, and knowing it has always made me a little nervous, as if I'm fated or genetically programmed to repeat what my father did at age forty-four. Is it possible I inherited his depressive nature and that at forty-four I'll be driven by pain and despair to end it all?

For years I've said that when I'm forty-four I'll be in therapy because I'm afraid of that ominous number. A couple of years back, when I was thirty-four, I decided to get a head start and began seeing a therapist. With any luck, I thought, I'll greet forty-four with a sense of triumph rather than impending doom.

The fact is that there is no clear agreement on why family members are at greater risk of suicide. Grief and the depression that may follow a suicide (or any death, for that matter) are certainly contributing factors. Genetics may be involved, since depression and schizophrenia, which put people at greater risk of taking their own lives, can be passed on through genetic material. And then there's the example set by someone who commits suicide. In other words, "If this is how my father or sister or husband dealt with his or her problems, maybe it's an option for me, too." I always remind myself that not choosing suicide is an option as well, and a far more constructive one at that.

On the flip side, I also think that the suicide of a loved one can be a deterrent—or an antidote—to suicide and suicidal thoughts. In moments when I've thought about suicide, such thoughts are instantly followed by the thought, *Given what my father did, I could never do that to my family.*

○ *Can you come to terms with the suicide of a loved one?*

Yes, over time you can come to terms with the loss of a loved one to suicide, but the fact that your loved one chose suicide is something you never forget.

And there are plenty of reminders. Inevitably, your loved one will come up in conversation. Also there are anniversaries, birthdays, and holidays. For years I got depressed around the time of year when my father died, but it wasn't until a decade after his death that I made any connection between the depression and my father's suicide. During the first few years, Father's Day was the worst. All the other kids at school talked about what they were getting their fathers, and all I could do was joke that I was lucky I didn't have to worry about that.

For other people, the worst time of year may be Christmas or Thanksgiving. For still others, a specific event such as a college graduation or a wedding may trigger that acute sense that someone is missing.

It's a cliché to say that time heals all wounds, but even in the case of suicide, *as long as you deal with the experience and don't bury it,* in time you will feel better. Eventually, you'll even be able to talk about the experience without feeling that someone is ripping your guts out.

○ *How long does it take to get over the suicide of a loved one?*

I don't know if you ever "get over" the suicide of a loved one. That's a phrase that implies that it's over and done. Finished. Book closed. The end. A better question would be, "How long will I *grieve* over the suicide of my loved one?" And add to that, "How long will it take to *accept* the suicide of my loved one?"

This is not something you put behind you in six months. Even people who have been through the death of a loved one from an accident or natural causes aren't usually through grieving so quickly. In these cases, after an initial period of intense grief lasting weeks or months, it is perfectly normal for people to grieve for a year to a year and a half or more. Fully accepting the loss takes even longer.

In the case of suicide, the whole process will almost always take longer, because before you can accept what's happened, you first have to deal with what it is that *did* happen. For example, when someone dies of a stroke, you know what happened. In all likelihood there isn't anyone to blame and you're not feeling guilty that you didn't do enough to prevent the death. You can move right through the process of grieving without getting caught up in a variety of emotions that can keep you from ever fully accepting the death of your loved one.

I wish I could say there was a clear-cut answer to this question—as in, "After one year you will feel . . . "—but there isn't. I've interviewed people who were able to get through their grief and accept the suicide of their loved one in just a couple of years. For me, it was more than two decades before I even had all the details of what happened.

There is no formula to calculate how long the grieving process should last or how long it will take to accept the suicide death of a loved one. Circumstances are different. People are different. But if you or someone you love seems unable to get past his or her initial grief, and acceptance seems like an impossibility, it is important for the person who is grieving to get help from a support group or mental-health professional.

○ *What kind of help can people get in dealing with a suicide?*

The first thing to know is that there is plenty of help to be had and that it's available in different forms.

For people who like to read, there are books and articles on the subject of suicide available through your local library or bookstore. In researching *Why Suicide?* I've read a lot about suicide and its aftermath that has helped me better understand what my father did, as well as my reactions and the reactions of my family members. It's been a comfort to learn that I'm hardly the only one who has been through this and that the ways in which I responded to my father's death were perfectly normal. I'm not crazy after all.

Not everyone likes to read, and most often reading isn't enough. Talking about your experience can be extremely helpful. You can talk to a school counselor, a member of the clergy, or a psychologist, psychiatrist, or social worker. You can also call a suicide hot line, or perhaps, most important, start attending a support group for people who have lived through the suicide of a loved one.

○ *What can my family do to cope with a suicide?*

Talk with one another. Ask questions. Don't hide your feelings. Go to a counselor and/or support group. And take your kids with you. There is no need for your family to experience the lasting hurt and isolation that mine did.

○ *Why do people feel the need to keep secret the suicide of a loved one?*

Given that we generally look at suicide as something shameful and embarrassing, keeping it a secret seems like the natural thing to do, whether the motive is to protect ourselves, our children, and/or our deceased loved one from judgment and criticism. In purely material terms, if there is the fear that a life-insurance policy could be voided, some people may feel compelled to hide the true cause of death. For more on life insurance, see chapter 1, "The Basics."

○ *Why not just keep it a secret? Why talk about it?*

If you don't talk about the suicide, you can't come to terms with it. If you can't come to terms with it, it will burden you in some way for the rest of your life.

There's another reason not to keep suicide a secret. There is still tremendous stigma attached to any suicide. By keeping it secret, nothing will change and you will passively contribute to the stigmatization of your loved one, yourself, and ultimately your children. Nothing will change if we refuse to make that change happen ourselves. Telling the truth can be frightening. It can be embarrassing. It can be awkward. You can never be certain how someone will react. But if we hang on to the secret and never give people the chance to learn, understand, and grow, the stigma of suicide will poison our lives for generations to come.

I like Alison's attitude in dealing with her child, Rachel. From the very beginning, she told her daughter the truth about her father's suicide. "I didn't want her to feel this was something that she had to hide, that she had to be ashamed of. Because she was four, she didn't know anything about the stigma of suicide, and I wanted to help her avoid that burden. As she's grown older, she's learned from others how difficult this whole issue is. I've worried a lot about how she would handle it. But I don't think I have to worry. Next year she starts middle school, and she's told me how she wants to start her own support group for other kids like her. That gives me hope." That should give us all hope.

○ *How can therapy and support groups for people coping with suicide help?*

For many if not most people who have experienced the suicide of a loved one, talking—about their experience, their feelings, their anguish—helps, whether it's in the context of one-on-one therapy with a psychologist or psychiatrist or a support group specifically for people dealing with suicide.

Donna Morrish, a family therapist and clinical consultant for San Francisco Suicide Prevention, is a big proponent of support groups. "I think the groups are very beneficial. If I was forced to choose between individual counseling and a group, I'd take the group every time. For one thing, being with a group of people who have been through the same thing works to dissolve the stigma. Here you are, sitting with this group of perfectly nice people, and the same thing happened to them.

Also, people who have been through a suicide feel so alienated and isolated, and experience subtle blame. In this group you can talk about all of this, and there are people who can identify with what you're going through."

Another advantage of a group, she explained, is that there's a mix of people. Some are new and are just beginning to deal with their feelings, and others are further along. "So the new people can see a path," Morrish said. "If you can see that people come through their grief, then it gives the griever some courage."

Getting help isn't just for people who have recently experienced a suicide. I can personally testify that you can talk about it with a therapist twenty-three years after the fact—as I did—and benefit enormously from the experience of understanding what you've been through, why you feel the way you do, and how your loved one's suicide has affected your life.

Alison didn't take her daughter, Rachel, for any kind of professional help until six years after her husband committed suicide. "I had some concerns over the years that she never really cried much about what happened to her father, but I just assumed she'd dealt with it well." Then last summer Rachel was watching a television show where one of the characters died. "It was the grandparent, and Rachel became hysterical. The emotion came out for the first time, and she really cried."

After that experience, Alison enrolled herself and Rachel in a bereavement program run by a local hospice. "There were six children in Rachel's group, and they were all about the same age and had all lost a parent. The person leading the group taught them that they were allowed to express their feelings. So the children talked together about how this made them feel. It was great because it was the one place where they didn't feel different from other kids. They all had a parent die. The counselor told me several weeks into this that she thought Rachel had dealt well with the death of her father and was helping some of the other kids get through their grief."

○ *What happens at a support group for people coping with the suicide of a loved one?*

More than anything, people talk. The group may be organized and run by people who have experienced the suicide of a loved one, or it may be organized through a local hospital or mental-health center and run by a mental-health professional.

Carolyn, whose son shot himself, started a support group several years ago in an attempt to come to terms with her son's death. The monthly meetings, which are held at a local hospital, draw anywhere from a handful to three dozen people. "We have people from every walk of life, every profession, and all ages from fourteen on up. At the start of the meeting I introduce myself and explain what the support group is about and that everything said in the room stays there. Confidentiality is very important in making people feel comfortable to speak honestly. Then we go around the room—people are seated in chairs arranged in a circle—and people introduce themselves and briefly talk about their circumstances. Some people are in such pain that they can't yet talk about it, and so they simply listen to the discussion."

There is nothing mysterious or exotic about these support groups. They're simply a place where people can gather to talk about what they've been through, share their feelings, and help one another cope with their experiences and begin the difficult process of healing.

○ *Does everyone need the help of a psychologist or support group to cope with a suicide?*

There are plenty of people who have managed to cope with the suicide of a loved one without seeing a counselor or going to a support group. And I know there are experts who believe it's not necessary. Nonetheless, I think it's essential, especially for children and young people, who don't have the same coping skills and support networks that adults have. Even for adults who are doing a good job of coping, seeing a counselor or joining a support group can only help speed the healing process. And what could be bad about that?

○ *What do you say to someone who asks how your loved one died?*

Rachel, who is now ten years old, says, "My father committed suicide when I was four." Her mother told me: "That's the easy part for her. The part she hates is when people say in response, 'I'm sorry.' I asked her why she hated that, and she said, 'Mommy, they didn't do anything wrong, so why are they saying they're sorry?'" Alison asked Rachel what she thought people should say and Rachel said, "They should say, 'I can't imagine how you felt.'"

Telling the truth flat out—for example, "He committed suicide"—is very difficult for many people. It gets easier the more you do it, but there are still times I take a deep breath when someone I've recently met gets around to questions about my family. I can always see it coming. It usually goes something like this:

Are your parents both still alive?
No, my father died years ago.

How old were you?
I was twelve.

He must have been very young.
He was. He was only forty-four.

Did he have a heart attack?
No, he committed suicide.

Invariably that revelation is greeted with some form of surprise and on rare occasion discomfort. Usually people will say, "That must have been terrible for you." And these days I say, "Yes, it was terrible." I used to say, "Well, it was a long time ago," attempting to discount the impact and move away from the subject. I still don't like to dwell on it, but I no longer feel the need to discount what happened and its impact on my life.

○ **What is a suicide survivor or survivor of suicide?**

Before I started work on this book, I thought a suicide survivor was someone who had survived a suicide attempt. In fact, it's the phrase I hear—and read—that's most often used to describe someone who has lived through the suicide of a loved one.

I've never thought of myself as someone who "survived" a suicide. I feel I've coped with and learned to live with the reality of what my father did and how it affected my family and my life. And, of course, I did survive the experience. I'm here all these years later, still wrestling with and talking about it. But to me being called a suicide survivor feels like I'm being condescended to, like a happy face is being pasted on a reality that isn't nearly so heroic or hopeful as the term *survivor* might suggest. I feel more like a victim of my father's suicide.

○ *What books do you recommend for people coping with the suicide of a loved one?*

Please see the appendix for recommended books.

○ *How do I find a local support group for people who have lived through the suicide of a loved one?*

There are a number of ways to find such a group. One of them is to contact the American Association of Suicidology (its address and phone number are listed in the appendix) and ask for a referral to a local survivors' support group. You can also call a local crisis telephone line or suicide hot line (check the appendix or your local phone book, or call directory assistance for the number). Or call your local community mental-health center. Don't put it off. *Call now.*

CHAPTER 8

ASSISTED
SUICIDE

What is assisted suicide?

Assisted suicide is one of the most fraught emotional, political, and moral issues of our time. Only abortion and gay rights are guaranteed to generate more heat and hysteria. So what is everyone so riled up about? I'm going to do my best to explain.

In it's simplest terms, an assisted suicide is a circumstance where one person helps another commit suicide. But when people talk about assisted suicide, what they're usually referring to is a situation in which a terminally ill person asks for and receives help from a loved one or doctor to end his or her life. That help can come in a variety of forms, from providing a lethal dose of medication to administering the drug to simply being present at the time of the suicide for emotional support.

○ *How about an example?*

I can give a personal example, because several years ago I was asked by a friend who was in the late stages of brain cancer to assist him in ending his life. I'll never forget the moment when he called me to his bedside and told me what he wanted. He was bedridden and had difficulty speaking, and he explained that he didn't want to spend the last days of his life in a hospital, unconscious and hooked up to bottles, tubes, and machines. He was determined to die at home, with his wife and young son with him, and he wanted to choose the time. He feared that if he didn't do it soon, he'd slip into a coma and linger in a vegetative state, which was absolutely the last thing he wanted for himself or his family. He'd already talked to his wife about his wish to die, but, he explained to me, he didn't want her to have to deal with this on her own, which was why he asked for my help.

I was already grief-stricken over my close friend's impending death, and the prospect of his dying any sooner, with or without my help, upset me even more. I listened closely to what he had to say, and the gravity of his request made my heart pound. I told him that I understood what he was saying and that I would talk with his wife.

Later in this chapter I'll explain how we reached a decision and what we did.

○ *Is assisted suicide the same thing as doctor-assisted suicide?*

As the term suggests, in a doctor-assisted suicide it's the doctor who provides the requested assistance, whether that assistance comes in the form of advice, prescribed medication, or the injection of a fatal dose of a drug—morphine, for example.

○ *Are there other names for assisted and doctor-assisted suicide?*

I think *assisted suicide* and *doctor-assisted suicide* work just fine as phrases to describe what we're talking about. But not everyone agrees with me. So here are just a few phrases I came across that are used by everyone—from proponents of assisted suicide to its opponents: *self-deliverance, self-enacted death, assisted dying, physician aid-in-dying, aid-in-dying, accelerated death,* and *physician-assisted death.*

○ *Is euthanasia the same as assisted suicide?*

When I hear the word *euthanasia* I imagine something sinister, like Adolf Hitler and his systematic program to exterminate mentally and physically handicapped people in Germany. Hitler used the word *euthanasia* to describe what was in fact the mass murder of approximately one hundred thousand men, women, and children.

By definition, euthanasia is simply the act of killing for reasons of mercy. What comes to mind for me is a scene from a movie where a mortally wounded soldier begs his buddy to shoot him to end his suffering and the buddy reluctantly agrees, knowing it is the merciful thing to do.

What gets confusing is that, depending upon who you're talking to and what country you're from, euthanasia can mean different things and can be used to convey different messages.

In Holland, for example, the word *euthanasia* is used without sinister overtones to describe a doctor hastening the death of a terminally ill patient on the request of that patient by administering a fatal dose of medication. This is considered different from *physician-assisted suicide*, which is the term used in Holland to describe a circumstance in which a doctor provides the medication for the patient to end his life but the patient himself takes the fatal overdose. In that case the doctor is only *assisting* in the suicide.

For those who use the word *euthanasia* as it is used in Holland, there is usually a distinction made between "voluntary" and "involuntary" euthanasia. With voluntary euthanasia, a person asks a doctor to help him or her die, and the doctor administers the fatal dose of drugs. With involuntary euthanasia, a doctor administers a fatal dose of drugs without having been asked to do so by the patient.

In the United States, *assisted suicide* is generally taken to include both voluntary euthanasia and assisted suicide as I've described them above. So whether a doctor injects a fatal dose of drugs at a patient's request, a friend provides the fatal dose of pills, or a daughter holds the hand of her mother while her mother swallows a fatal dose of medication, we usually describe what occurs as an assisted suicide.

What can get really confusing is that sometimes you'll see the word *euthanasia* used by those who oppose doctor-assisted suicide to give the whole debate sinister overtones. In other words, their argument runs, if we allow assisted suicide, before we know it doctors will be "euthanizing" the infirm and handicapped, just like Hitler did. But others, like the author Andrew Solomon, who in the May 22, 1995, issue of the *New Yorker* wrote eloquently of his mother's death, use the word *euthanasia* in the same way the Dutch do.

In this chapter I generally don't use the word *euthanasia*. I include under the single term *assisted suicide* those circumstances in which a person gets the assistance in dying he or she has *asked for* from a doctor or any other person, whatever

p 151 ¶ 6 - N.H.

44 - seratonin

form it takes—whether it's just a prescription or the actual lethal injection.

○ *Is assisted suicide the same thing as the "right to die" issue?*

In recent years, the phrase *right to die* has been used to describe a broad range of end-of-life issues, including assisted suicide; the withdrawal of life-sustaining treatment, such as respirators; the refusal of medical treatment on religious grounds; and the refusal of medical treatment by terminally ill patients. Despite this umbrella meaning, many people, as well as the press, frequently use *right to die* as shorthand for *assisted suicide.*

Historically, those concerned with the "right to die" issue have focused more specifically on the right of people to refuse medical treatment in the end stages of life. Remember the Karen Ann Quinlan case back in the mid-1970s? Karen Ann Quinlan fell into an irreversible coma after accidentally overdosing on Quaaludes and alcohol. She was being kept alive with the help of a respirator. Though Karen Ann could no longer make decisions for herself about her medical care, her parents believed she would not want to be kept alive in a vegetative state by artificial means.

After consulting with their doctors and priest, Karen Ann's parents decided to ask to have the respirator removed. The hospital refused, and the case wound up in court. The ensuing battle, which was finally decided in the New Jersey Supreme Court, sparked a national debate over the "right to die" and inspired state legislatures across the United States to consider "living will" laws. Living wills or "advance directives" allow you to state in a legal document your wishes regarding the use of life-sustaining medical treatment in the event you become ill and can't make decisions for yourself.

This is a subject my grandmother and I have talked about many times, in relation to ourselves, and in relation to my grandfather when he was in the last months of his life. We both agreed that we wouldn't want to be kept alive by tubes and machines, and we've both filled out living wills to make sure that doesn't happen.

Even though my grandfather didn't fill out a living will before becoming incapacitated, my grandmother stated emphatically to his doctors that he was not to be kept alive by artificial means. It was a very painful decision for her, but after sixty-five years of marriage, she knew that it was a decision he would have made himself if he'd been able to. The doctors honored her wishes.

Karen Ann Quinlan's parents won their case, and in May 1976 her respirator was removed. Unexpectedly, Karen Ann continued breathing on her own and lived until 1985, when she died of pneumonia. She remained in a coma during those nine years and was fed through a nasogastric tube.

○ *Why do people choose assisted suicide?*

The vast majority of people who ask a friend or doctor for help in dying are facing a terminal illness. In a 1990 Dutch study of people who chose to hasten their deaths, 85 percent were cancer patients; the rest included those suffering from AIDS and multiple sclerosis. All of the patients were in the final stages of their illnesses.

Terminally ill people who choose assisted suicide offer a variety of reasons for wanting to hasten their deaths, including the following:

○ I'm afraid of the suffering and potential indignity.

◦ I don't want to suffer (physical pain, nausea, difficulty with breathing, side effects of medication, etc.) anymore.

◦ I want to die while I still have my wits about me.

◦ I don't want to live if I can't control my bodily functions.

◦ I don't want to be a burden to my loved ones (financially or physically).

◦ I don't want to spend my last days in a hospital.

For my friend who asked me to help him die, his primary concerns were incontinence and the possibility of slipping into a coma and lingering for days or weeks before dying. He was a man who had always been in control of his life, and not being able to control his body made him furious. Furthermore, the last thing he wanted his family to do was keep vigil as he slowly slipped away. In the end he didn't have a choice about whether he was going to die, but he was determined to decide how and when.

◦ *Aren't these people just depressed or suffering from pain that isn't being properly treated? Can't they be helped by counseling, antidepressants, and painkillers?*

Plenty of terminally ill people, perhaps most, who express a desire to hasten their deaths are not receiving proper treatment for pain or for depression. This is one of the major arguments raised by those who oppose legalized doctor-assisted suicide — that those who receive inadequate care will be the most likely to ask for help in hastening their death. A patient's outlook may be altered considerably by proper pain management and treatment for depression. But that's not the case with everyone. There are people for whom this is a rational decision, as it was for my friend. He wasn't depressed. His pain was under control. But the end was near, and he didn't want it drawn out. His desire to hasten his death was absolutely consistent with who he was. I think my friend, his wife, and I could have benefited from talking with a professional counselor about the whole thing, but, knowing that assisted suicide is illegal, we couldn't risk talking to anyone about it, not even my friend's doctor.

○ *Besides people who are terminally ill, who else chooses assisted suicide?*

Although the vast majority of people who choose assisted suicide have terminal illnesses, some of those who ask for help in dying are chronically ill or infirm and/or suffer from depression.

One of the most shocking stories I came across in researching assisted suicide concerned a Dutch psychiatrist who actually helped a patient of his who was depressed—but otherwise physically healthy—commit suicide. Dr. Boudewijn Chabot gave sleeping pills to a fifty-year-old woman who had asked him to help her commit suicide because she had lost the will to live after a failed marriage and the deaths of her two sons. Even more surprising, the Supreme Court of the Netherlands ruled in June 1994 that the doctor should not be punished for helping his patient end her mental suffering.

While the story of Dr. Chabot is by far the rare exception, it illustrates exactly the kind of situation that opponents of legalized doctor-assisted suicide point to as an indication of what could happen if U.S. laws were changed to permit doctor-assisted suicide.

○ *Why do people have to ask for help? Why not do it themselves?*

Plenty of people who are facing terminal illness take their own lives without help from anyone, but many people in the late stages of a terminal illness don't have the physical and/or emotional wherewithal to do the research and find the means to end their lives on their own, without the assistance of a loved one or doctor. Besides, how many of us would want to end our lives without the support and presence of those who love us? I know I wouldn't.

For my friend, it was simply too late for him to do it himself. I know he didn't want to put me or his wife at risk, but he was too ill to do the work required to find out how to end his life, and was far too ill to get the drugs he needed. He was even too weak to hold the cup of water he needed to swallow the pills. But these weren't the only reasons he didn't do it himself. He knew this was what he wanted to do, but he was scared. Who wouldn't be? So, besides the practical help he needed, he was counting on his wife and me for emotional support.

○ *How many assisted suicides are there each year?*

No one knows how many assisted suicides there are in the United States each year. Almost all are kept secret. But we do know that in Holland, a government-appointed panel estimated that in 1990 there were approximately twenty-three hundred cases of voluntary euthanasia and four hundred cases of physician-assisted suicide (where the doctor simply provided the fatal dose of medication) in a population of about 14.5 million.

The Reverend Ralph Mero, a Unitarian minister who is the executive director of Compassion in Dying, an organization that provides assistance to terminally ill patients who wish to hasten the end of their lives, estimates that there are about fifty thousand cases of assisted suicide in the United States each year. While Mero's estimate is in line with the Dutch numbers (when applied to the U.S. population), there are those who believe that the actual figure is much lower and that the Dutch statistics aren't applicable because assisted suicide and voluntary euthanasia are not nearly as well accepted a practice in the United States as they are in the Netherlands.

Whatever the true number, we know that there are thousands, or perhaps tens of thousands, of people each year who ask for help in dying and get it.

○ *Is the assisted-suicide issue a new one?*

No. Although the very public and heated nationwide debate over assisted suicide is relatively new, the practice of assisted suicide is at least as old as the Parthenon. In ancient Greece, "physicians who believed a case was hopeless routinely suggested suicide and often supplied the lethal drugs with which to accomplish it." (Colt, p. 356)

A little closer to home, in seventeenth-century Brittany, "a person suffering from an incurable disease might apply to the parish priest for the Holy Stone. If the priest agreed, the family gathered, prayers were said, and the Stone was brought down upon the person's head, often by the oldest person in the village." (Colt, p. 356)

In the United States, a bill proposing legalization of "euthanasia for incurable sufferers who wished to die" was introduced into the Ohio legislature in 1906. It was defeated. Thirty years later, a bill sponsored by the Voluntary Euthanasia Society of London that would have allowed terminally ill people to apply for euthanasia was defeated in Parliament. (Colt, p. 357)

○ **Why has assisted suicide become such a big issue in recent years?**

Several trends have led to today's public debate. One is autonomy in patient care. There's a growing public awareness that doctors are not gods and that all of us need to take more responsibility for making decisions about our own medical care.

A second trend concerns the fact that there are more of us who are living longer. Part of that has to do with demographics; as the baby boom generation ages, it will greatly expand the ranks of old people. And part of that has to do with the fact that medical advances are keeping more of us alive longer. Unfortunately, medical technologies that successfully extend life don't necessarily make that life worth living, forcing many people to decide whether those technologies should be withdrawn, or even used in the first place.

The third and overriding trend is the general concern over how as a society we're going to handle the events at the end of life. Dr. Thomas A. Preston, a cardiologist who is a professor of medicine at the University of Washington and a medical adviser to Compassion in Dying, dates this trend back two decades. "That's when the issue of 'do not resuscitate' began. When we first considered not resuscitating everyone, there were people who said this was murder. Now it's taken entirely for granted that we don't resuscitate absolutely everyone. That was followed by the more heated debate over the withdrawal of life-sustaining technologies. At first this was thought of by some doctors and ethicists as killing, because when a doctor removes a ventilator, this is an act that leads to death. It's a passive act, but it leads to death. Now doctors have come to understand that they are not killing people, but allowing them to die."

Preston sees the current debate over assisted suicide as a natural evolution of these social trends in medicine. "Patients today are aware that they have both the right and the obligation to become involved in how and when they die. It seems like a natural consequence that people would take the next step and say, 'If I'm riddled with cancer and suffering, why should I just wait around? Why shouldn't I be able to control my death and end my life at home with pills?'"

○ *Is assisted suicide against the law?*

Yes, which is the biggest reason anyone involved in assisting in a suicide is likely to keep it secret. More than half the states and the District of Columbia have specific statutes that prohibit anyone from assisting in a suicide. In the remaining states, those who assist in a suicide can be prosecuted under the homicide and manslaughter statutes.

There could be one exception, depending upon how things go in the courts. In 1994, Oregon voters approved a ballot initiative permitting doctor-assisted suicide according to specific guidelines. But before the new law could go into effect it was challenged in court. Until that dispute is settled, those who assist in a suicide are not protected from possible prosecution anywhere in the United States.

○ *Can you get in trouble if you assist in a suicide?*

Yes, but there are several reasons criminal prosecutions are uncommon relative to the estimated number of assisted suicides. First, most people who participate in an assisted suicide remain silent. Second, the patient is in the final stages of terminal illness, so the death is expected. And third, as long as nonviolent means are used, the death appears natural, so suspicions aren't aroused. Even if there is suspicion on the part of the doctor and/or coroner, he or she is likely to look the other way. And any doctor who provides assistance will undoubtedly report the death as being from natural causes.

Not every circumstance is typical. Rev. Ralph Mero warns, "If a gun goes off, someone's going to get arrested. There have been several prosecutions where people provided firearms to persons who wanted to end their lives."

If the authorities are made aware of an assisted suicide, they may feel pressure to investigate, depending on the underlying health of the patient, the voluntariness of the death, and the motives of the person who is assisting. But prosecutors seem reluctant to pursue these cases because a jury's sympathies are likely to be with the defendant. Even when the law has been broken, as long as it's clear that the patient was terminally ill, the assistance was requested, and the person assisting was motivated by a desire to help end suffering, juries are unlikely to render a guilty verdict.

○ *Can you give an example of someone who was arrested for assisting in a suicide?*

One of the more celebrated and heartbreaking cases in recent years that led to an arrest involved a man who helped his terminally ill and beloved eighty-eight-year-old father end his life. William F. Meyer III, a sales and marketing executive and a respected community leader in Westport, Connecticut, told *Connecticut* magazine how he assisted his father, William F. Meyer, Jr., in ending his life. This led local authorities to charge him with second-degree manslaughter.

Meyer's father had been suffering from colon and lung cancer for ten years, and he made clear to his son (who prefers to be called Bill) that he wanted to end his suffering and his life.

The father begged his son for help, and Bill, who was extremely close to his father, agreed.

First Bill and his father read *Final Exit,* a controversial book about how to commit suicide, and then talked to the father's doctor, who reluctantly agreed to prescribe a sedative so that the father would be asleep when the oxygen in the plastic bag he planned to use to suffocate himself ran out. (For more information on *Final Exit,* see chapter 2, "How?")

The first attempt failed when Bill's father instinctively pulled the bag off his head before suffocating. Bill had left his father after making certain the bag was secure—so as not to be implicated in what was supposed to look like an unassisted suicide—and when he came back, the bag was off and his father was very much alive.

The second time around, Bill watched his father swallow a dozen prescription sleeping pills, and then he helped him put the plastic bag over his head and secure it with rubber bands. He planned to stay long enough to make certain his father did not remove the bag.

The sleeping pills knocked Meyer out, but again he instinctively tried to remove the bag. This time, as Bill told *Connecticut* magazine, "I held his hands back. He kept reaching up. He kept trying to take the bag off. Like when someone's drowning, you know how they struggle? They throw their arms up because they're going down for the third time. It's because you're losing oxygen and you're gasping for breath. You fight to stay alive. He struggled for about five minutes."

Bill knew he was risking arrest by going public with his story, but as he explained to me when I interviewed him by telephone, the last thing his father told him before he died was "See you someday. Tell my story." Bill said, "My father was always a civic leader—in 1985, the Town Council of West Hartford declared a William F. Meyer Appreciation Day for all of his volunteer contributions to the town—and he felt that by my telling his story he could help other people who were in similar situations. He would have been upset to know that I was arrested for following his wishes, but he would have been delighted to know the impact his story had."

Bill's case was never actually tried before a jury. "After my arrest," he said,"my lawyer told me that I could apply for a program called 'accelerated rehabilitation.' It's a program that was enacted by the Connecticut legislature for people who have never been charged with a crime before. It involves no admission of guilt and not only does it result in no conviction, but your arrest is erased retroactively."

A key element of applying for the accelerated-rehabilitation program is finding community support and character references. That was one part Bill didn't have to worry about. "More than 130 people wrote to the judge, including seven ministers and five doctors, who served as character references." Bill also got editorial backing from the *Hartford Courant*, the second-largest newspaper in New England, and the *Westport News*.

At the hearing itself, six people, in addition to Bill's lawyer, spoke for him, and Bill spoke for himself. And, of course, the district attorney made his case. Bill recalled, "He made a very passionate appeal to the judge that I should go to trial, but in the end the judge wasn't convinced. While the judge admonished me for what I did, on December 14, 1994, he granted the accelerated rehabilitation, the first time in Connecticut's history that anybody charged with a major felony had been granted accelerated rehabilitation."

During the two years of the rehabilitation period, Bill has to call his probation officer four times. There were also two special conditions to the agreement. First, he had to make a one-thousand-dollar contribution in his father's name to the Connecticut prisoners' youth program. Second, he had to agree not to assist or help in any other suicides.

Bill considers the court's decision to be "a real victory for self-determination [i.e., assisted suicide] for somebody who is terminally ill."

○ *Did Bill Meyer have any regrets about what he did?*

I thought he might, so I asked him. But he said, "I had regrets initially when they arrested me and put me in jail for three hours, but then when I walked out of jail and there were three television crews and four newspaper reporters waiting for me, I knew I could make a difference. My attorney told me not to say anything, that I'd put myself in jail if I talked to the reporters, but I felt that I did the compassionate, loving thing and that if there was a loving God and justice, I wouldn't go to jail."

Bill Meyer has had many opportunities to tell his father's story. In addition to all the local media attention, he landed on the front page of the *New York Times* and was featured on *60 Minutes, Donahue*, and the *Today* show.

○ *What are the arguments for legalizing doctor-assisted suicide?*

Those who argue in favor of legalizing doctor-assisted suicide generally believe that terminally ill people have the right to seek humane assistance in dying through medication prescribed and/or administered by a personal physician under stringent clinical supervision. Beyond this general belief, the following are the more specific points made by some of those who support legalized doctor-assisted suicide:

○ Competent terminally ill people have the constitutional right to enlist a willing doctor's help in killing themselves. That was the opinion reached by Federal District Court Judge Barbara Rothstein in Seattle in May 1994 when she struck down a 140-year-old Washington State law that barred assisted suicide. Judge Rothstein's ruling was later reversed.

○ By denying terminally ill people the right to end their lives, we prolong their suffering by trying to keep them alive with surgery, drugs, and machines.

○ "Making a person die in a way that others approve, but that affronts his own dignity, is a serious, unjustified, unnecessary form of tyranny." So states Ronald Dworkin in his book *Life's Dominion: An Argument About Abortion and Euthanasia*.

○ Doctors have a moral obligation to help patients end their suffering, including helping them die if their suffering is unbearable and irreversible.

○ If doctor-assisted suicide is permitted, terminally ill patients will feel less pressure to end their lives prematurely. As the laws stand now, you can't ask your doctor to administer a lethal injection. If you want to end your life, you still have to be able to physically do it. As Dr. M. Gregg Steadman wrote in the spring 1993 issue of *Northern California Update*, a newsletter published by the Hemlock Society of Northern California, "Those of us who may be told that our illness cannot be cured by modern medicine and who then may visualize a progressive disabling, painful end may turn to suicide while we are physically able. If we had a compassionate physician who would encourage us to tolerate suffering as long as possible and assured us relief if we began to find life intolerable, suicide could be set aside. It is the fear of helpless, intolerable misery that leads to suicide."

○ People are already asking for and getting assistance in dying. By regulating assisted suicide and making it a part of overall health care, we can better ensure that those who desire aid in dying get proper counseling. And if assistance is deemed appropriate, that assistance can be given by trained medical professionals who know what they're doing.

○ By denying the terminally ill the right to seek aid in dying from a doctor, we force laypeople to act on their own, risking additional pain and suffering in the event the assisted suicide is botched. And we force some terminally ill people into using extraordinary means to end their lives, such as guns and other violent methods, because they don't have access to proper advice and/or the appropriate drugs.

○ *What are the arguments against legalizing doctor-assisted suicide?*

Given the intensity of the debate over legalizing doctor-assisted suicide, it can be difficult to clearly hear the various and often compelling opinions of people who oppose legalization. The opinions that follow range from those based on moral and religious grounds to those expressing concern regarding the preparedness of health-care professionals to deal with the practical aspects of helping people die.

○ The broadest argument and most convincing, for me, against legalized doctor-assisted suicide is that we are way ahead of ourselves. First, assisted suicide is just one part of the larger debate on how we're going to care for people at the end of their lives. And until we resolve how to give equitable and appropriate care to people at the end of their lives (not to mention during their lives), we can't talk about providing something as socially, morally, and practically complex as doctor-assisted suicide.

○ Second, the public isn't yet adequately educated about the choices at the end of life, so how can people be expected to make informed decisions about assisted suicide? And doctors themselves are not properly trained to deal with end-of-life issues or the practical aspects of helping a patient die.

○ Assistance in dying will be subject to the same inequities and biases as other areas of health care. Those who can pay for private care already get better treatment than those who can't. Will poor patients get the proper counseling? Will their pain be treated adequately so they aren't compelled to seek assisted suicide as an alternative to suffering? Will terminally ill older people receive the same encouragement to continue living as younger patients?

○ Perhaps the most emotionally charged argument against legalizing doctor-assisted suicide is that it will start us down a slippery slope. Once we let doctors help terminally ill patients end their lives, there's the possibility that some doctors will abuse that right and euthanize sick, old, or unwanted people who don't really want to die but whose care is expensive or burdensome.

○ Family members and/or doctors will pressure the terminally ill because of the expense or burden of caring for them. Or family members will pressure doctors for these same reasons to take an active role in ending a terminally ill relative's life.

○ If we legalize doctor-assisted suicide, terminally ill people whose treatment is expensive or burdensome to their families will feel guilty and decide they should choose assisted suicide for that reason.

○ Decisions to end life will likely be made in the privacy of a doctor's office or hospital room, so it will be impossible to make sure that proper guidelines are followed. The lack of oversight could lead to widespread abuse.

○ Assisted suicide is morally wrong, because whatever it's called, it's still one person killing another.

○ Doctors are supposed to "do no harm," so by assisting a patient in a suicide, a doctor is acting unethically.

○ By casting doctors in the role of killer rather than healer, we will destroy the trust people now have in them.

○ Men and women are made in the image and likeness of God, and destroying God's image is an offense against the Creator. Life, no matter how feeble or impaired, is a gift from God, and taking that life is against God's will.

The previous two sentences are drawn from statements made by the Catholic Church, which has been vehemently opposed to any effort to legalize assisted suicide. Interestingly, mainstream Protestant religions have remained virtually silent on this issue, with the exception of the Unitarian Universalists, who have endorsed the right of terminally ill people to end their lives.

○ If we did a better job of controlling the pain, discomfort, and depression of terminally ill patients, far fewer people would feel compelled to pursue assisted suicide.

○ By allowing people to end their lives before nature takes its course, we may be denying them and ourselves positive and enriching time together in the last months, weeks, days, or hours of their lives.

∘ Things should remain as they are, with doctors quietly assisting terminally ill patients in hastening their deaths. The threat of prosecution is the best safeguard against abuse, because as long as assisted suicide remains illegal, doctors will think more than twice before helping anyone except those patients who are in absolute need of such assistance.

∘ Rather than legalize assisted suicide, we should expand hospice care to give the terminally ill an alternative to ending their lives.

○ *What exactly is a hospice?*

I always thought that a hospice was a place, but it turns out that although this is true, *hospice* also refers to a philosophy of caregiving that's based on the acceptance of death. The goal of hospice is not to prolong life, but to alleviate physical and emotional suffering and maximize the quality of life remaining through appropriate medical treatment and counseling. Hospice care extends beyond the patient to include counseling and support for loved ones throughout the process of dying.

Most hospice care is given in the home, although there are also freestanding hospice facilities.

○ *What does the Oregon assisted-suicide law permit?*

Measure 16, Oregon's assisted-suicide ballot initiative, was approved by voters in November 1994 by a vote of 51 percent to 49 percent. Under the new law, which has been challenged in court and has yet to go into effect, patients with six months to live may ask a doctor to prescribe a lethal dose of drugs to end unbearable suffering. But there are conditions. At least two doctors must agree that the patient's condition is terminal, the patient has to request the drugs at least three times—the third request must be in writing—and only the patient can administer the drugs.

○ *What are some of the arguments against Measure 16?*

Other than the arguments against assisted suicide that I've already discussed, there are two provisions in the Oregon law that have drawn particularly heated criticism: how the law defines *terminally ill*, and the fact that doctors may only prescribe the drugs to be used in the assisted suicide and not actually administer the drug or assist the patient in any way.

The Oregon law defines *terminally ill* as "having six months to live," and two doctors must certify that this is the case. The problem with this provision, as more than one doctor has pointed out, is that it's not always easy to predict how long a patient has to live. Patients who are given six months to live often stay alive longer, which means there's the danger that doctors may help people end their lives when they could still have positive and meaningful time ahead of them.

The fact that doctors can only *prescribe* the fatal dose of medication has led Russel D. Ogden to call Measure 16 the "coat-hanger euthanasia bill." Ogden, a social worker in Vancouver, British Columbia, who has done one of the very rare studies on assisted suicide, said that the passage of Measure 16 "is like saying to women that they can have access to an abortion, but they have to do it themselves. I can think of no other form of health care that requires that." Ogden warns that in the event things go wrong, and physicians and/or family members are compelled to provide direct assistance, they'll be breaking the new law and will be subject to prosecution.

Ogden is also greatly concerned that the practice of helping someone die is still poorly understood. "We have an abundance of legal, medical, theological, moral, and ethical discussion, but a total paucity of literature that looks at the actual practice. Until we talk to the terminally ill and talk to the people involved in assisting their death, we'll continue to talk about this in a very safe and lofty manner, without looking at it with any grounding in reality."

○ *What are the kinds of regulations that proponents of legalized doctor-assisted suicide recommend?*

In general, the regulations or codes of conduct recommended for doctors who provide assistance in suicide are designed to avoid and minimize mistakes and abuses.

In his book *Death and Dignity: Making Choices and Taking Charge*, Dr. Timothy E. Quill, a physician at Genesee Hospital in Rochester, New York, suggests "potential clinical criteria" for physician-assisted suicide. Following is a brief summary of these criteria.

1. The patient must, of his own free will and at his own initiative, clearly and repeatedly request to die rather than continue suffering.

2. The patient's judgment must not be distorted. The patient must be capable of understanding the decision and its implications and consequences.

3. The patient must have a condition that is incurable, and associated with severe, unrelenting, intolerable suffering.

4. The physician must ensure that the patient's suffering and the request are not the result of inadequate comfort care.

5. Physician-assisted suicide should be carried out only in the context of a meaningful doctor-patient relationship.

6. Consultation with another experienced physician is required to ensure the voluntariness and rationality of the patient's request, the accuracy of the diagnosis and prognosis, and the full exploration of comfort-oriented alternatives.

7. Clear documentation to support each condition above is required.

Along with these recommended criteria, Quill discusses the methods used in physician-assisted suicide. He notes that because assisted suicide has been kept so secret and has not been thoroughly studied, we don't know much about "the most humane and effective" methods. He suggests that if there is a change in policy to allow physician-assisted suicide, information about methods should be shared and the effectiveness of each method carefully analyzed. He concludes: "The methods selected should be 100 percent effective, and should not contribute to further patient suffering."

In 1991, Quill wrote an article in the *New England Journal of Medicine* about his assistance in the suicide of a leukemia patient named Diane. Though he was investigated by state authorities, he was never charged with any crime.

○ *What are the laws in other countries regarding doctor-assisted suicide?*

Physician-assisted suicide is not explicitly legal anywhere in the world, with the exception of the Northern Territory of Australia. As reported in the *New York Times* by Philip Shenon on

July 28, 1995, the territorial parliament passed a new law in the spring of 1995 permitting doctors to assist in the suicide of a terminally ill patient. According to the article, it was expected that the first patients to make use of the law would do so by late 1995.

In the Northern Territory, which is twice the size of Texas and has a population of 160,000, "a patient whose illness has been diagnosed as terminal by two doctors can ask for death, usually by pill or lethal injection, to put an end to suffering. At least one of the doctors must have a background in psychiatry, and a patient must wait at least nine days—a 'cooling-off period'—before the request can be met."

Despite the very vocal opposition to the new law from the Australian Medical Association, the Catholic Church, Right to Life Australia, and other groups that oppose doctor-assisted suicide, "similar legislation is being considered in several other, more heavily populated provinces."

Doctor-assisted suicide is an issue around the world, where organizations of all kinds are working on making the practice legal. In fact, there's an organization for such organizations, called the World Federation of the Right to Die Societies.

Luis Gallop, who is on the federation's board of directors and edits its newsletter, said the federation has approximately thirty-four member organizations in more than twenty countries, including Australia, Belgium, Canada, England, Colombia, Finland, France, Germany, India, Israel, Japan, Luxembourg, the Netherlands, New Zealand, Norway, Scotland, South Africa, Spain, Sweden, Switzerland, and the United States.

○ *Isn't doctor-assisted suicide legal in Holland?*

No. Both assisted suicide and voluntary euthanasia (the Dutch distinguish between the two) are still technically illegal and punishable by jail terms. But of all the world's nations, the Netherlands has the least restrictive policy.

According to Dutch guidelines for assisted suicide and voluntary euthanasia, which were established in 1993, doctors can avoid prosecution for helping a patient die as long as they notify the authorities and provide documentation that a patient was terminally ill, was suffering unbearably, and had repeatedly asked to die.

For the ten years preceding passage of the new law, Dutch courts looked the other way and allowed doctors to help their patients die, as long as they followed guidelines almost identical to those that have now become law.

○ *Are doctors in the Netherlands allowed to actually administer the fatal drugs?*

Yes. As Sherwin B. Nuland explains in his remarkable book *How We Die*, "The usual method is for the physician to induce deep sleep with barbiturates and then to inject a muscle-paralyzing drug to cause cessation of breathing." Most physician-assisted suicides, Nuland notes, take place in the patient's home.

○ *What other methods are used in assisted suicide?*

In a doctor-assisted suicide, a fatal dose of medication is used, either ingested or injected. In assisted suicide without a doctor's involvement, people use every method imaginable, from suffocation to firearms.

○ *What should you do if someone asks you to assist in a suicide? What do you need to consider?*

The first thing you need to do is talk. After my friend asked me for help, I discussed the whole thing with his wife, and then we both sat down with him to talk about why he wanted to hasten his death. If I had known then what I know now about this issue, I would have known what questions to ask beyond why he wanted to end his life. I would have asked him, for example, what he was afraid of and if he could see any alternatives to hastening his death. We didn't call anybody for advice—we were too afraid of letting anyone else find out— but even if we had overcome our fear, we wouldn't have known whom to call.

Mostly, we just let my friend talk, and we accepted his wishes without challenging him. Even if I had known more, I doubt things would have turned out any differently—he was emphatic about what he wanted—but I would have felt better knowing that we had explored every possible angle, corner, and crevice before agreeing that assisted suicide was the best alternative.

In my friend's case, we knew there was nothing the doctor could do for him other than keep him comfortable as his illness took its course. He'd already told us that. But medical and/or psychological intervention can help, especially in the case of someone who is motivated to hasten death because of pain and/or depression. So it's important for the patient and those immediately involved to sit down with the doctor and discuss the various end-of-life options, including hospice care. And depending upon the doctor, you may be able to engage him or her in a conversation about assisted suicide, or even enlist the physician's help.

Educating yourself is key. Without a thorough understanding of end-of-life issues and assisted suicide, you can't make an informed decision about whether to give the help that's been asked of you.

If after asking all the appropriate questions, doing all the research, and searching your heart, you decide to help a loved one hasten his or her death, you need to consider that you'll be breaking the law and the potential risks involved. What if the assisted suicide becomes known to the authorities? Are you prepared to deal with the legal consequences? What if something goes wrong? Are you prepared to intervene?

You may also find that after asking the questions, doing the research, and searching your heart, you decide not to help.

○ *What do you need to know if you're thinking about assisted suicide for yourself?*

There are many things you need to know and consider if you're thinking about asking for help in dying. The first and most important question to ask is whether there are alternatives. Is there a way to make the time you have left more comfortable and potentially rewarding for you and those you love? You also need to consider your motives. Why do you want to do this? Is it something you really want to do, or are you feeling pressure from those around you?

End-of-life issues, including assisted suicide, are not the kinds of things to consider on your own. Talk them out with trusted friends and/or family, or with a counselor or your doctor. And get the information you need to make an informed decision.

If you go beyond the thinking stage and decide on assisted suicide, you need to be very well informed about the specifics of how to hasten your death, including what method to use and how to acquire the things you need to carry out your plan. You also need to consider who is going to help, when to do it, where to do it, and who will be with you when the end comes. If, for example, you arrange for your loved ones to leave after you ingest a fatal dose of medication, you need to also consider who will return to "discover" that you've died while they were out. And you need to make certain that you don't put those who assist you in a position where they can be held legally responsible for your death.

○ *What can go wrong?*

Given the current circumstances, where doctors routinely don't have direct involvement in assisting their terminally ill patients who want to end their lives, a lot can go wrong. Most laypeople have little if any experience with hastening the death of someone who is terminally ill, and despite the existence of a book like *Final Exit*, which purports to tell people how to commit suicide, it's not necessarily the kind of thing you can get right on the first try.

Even with a doctor's direct involvement, there are risks, primarily because doctors do not receive training in how to help their terminally ill patients hasten their deaths. Much remains to be learned about the whole process of dying and how to hasten it without causing the patient any discomfort or pain.

Russel Ogden, who wrote his master's thesis on assisted suicides among people with AIDS, found that half of thirty-four cases he examined were "bungled, in that the death did not proceed as the parties had planned or expected. Some very grisly things occurred."

In his study, Ogden documents what went wrong. In one case, Ogden told me, a terminally ill man had discussed with his friends his desire for them to help him end his life, but they never settled on the specifics of how they would do it. "The illness galloped along and they were suddenly faced with doing it right away or going to the hospital. They didn't have

access to lethal medication, so they went the violent route."
The patient slit his wrists as his friends looked on. In a similar
case, those assisting resorted to using a gun.

Five of the cases, Ogden said, involved an initially unsuccessful attempt at suffocation. "There was one case where the
patient came to after the plastic bag had been placed over his
head. Through the bag he said, 'Hey, guys, what's going on?'
They had to take the bag off, calm him down, give him more
sedatives, and then rebag him. Initially this was described to
me as a pleasant, calm, romantic death. But the man who told
me the story called me well after I'd submitted my thesis and
explained what really happened. He said he'd been afraid to
tell me the truth." In another case of suffocation, when the patient didn't die initially, his friends resorted to smothering him
with a cushion.

Ogden reported that many of the acts of what he calls euthanasia (and which I would call assisted suicide) took several
hours or longer to be completed. As Ogden related in his
paper, one of the participants explained: "We injected him
with massive amounts of morphine and he didn't die. We used
a month's supply of morphine in three days. We were triple-
dosing him every hour because the information we had was
that eventually the morphine would arrest his respiratory system." In this case, it took four days for the loved one to die.

One final story from Russel Ogden. After all the publicity
that followed the release of his study, Ogden heard from a
woman who told him the story of what happened with her
husband. "She told me that she'd written a letter to a radio
program during all the publicity about *Final Exit*'s publication, and in it she said, 'Before your radio audience gets the
impression that *Final Exit* is the panacea, let me tell you
about my experience.' She explained how she used prescrip-

tion medication from three different physicians, all of which her husband ingested, but after three days he was still alive, although he was unconscious. Finally, at her request, the man's physician came to the house, inserted into her husband's vein a syringe filled with potassium chloride. Then the physician left and then she had to depress the plunger to inject her husband. Potassium chloride will arrest the heart almost immediately and it's virtually impossible to detect. When she depressed the plunger and her husband went into a massive cardiac arrest, he twitched and thrashed before he died. There's a very easy way to prevent this from happening by using a paralytic drug to prevent the body from heaving and twitching, but even physicians don't know what they're doing." Despite her relief that her husband's suffering was over, the woman was traumatized by her experience.

Ogden explained that the biggest lesson he learned from talking with people who had been through the experience of assisting in suicides was that it can be extremely difficult to kill someone without a doctor's help, even if that person is at the end stages of life. "Even with AIDS patients in the late stages of the disease, whose bodies are ravaged, it can be extremely difficult because they are typically young, their hearts and lungs are strong, and they're accustomed to heavy doses of medication."

Ogden attributed many of the problems people experienced to a lack of familiarity with the methods, "so you wind up waking up or wind up vomiting the drugs before you've had a chance to fall asleep. Many used the wrong medications, which are not effective, and they think that just volume will work."

Some of the other problems people have faced in an assisted suicide have had to do with the terminally ill patient's health. In the late stages of illness, a patient may be unable to swallow or ingest much liquid, making it impossible for the person to take a fatal dose of medication.

In the case of my friend, he was well enough to swallow the medication, but his wife had to help him because he wasn't strong enough to hold the cup of water or lift his head. And, as Russel Ogden noted, death doesn't necessarily occur right away. After taking the medication, my friend fell into a deep sleep and then a coma, but he didn't die until two days later.

I realize that some of what you've just read is gruesome, but I believe we should all be aware that assisting in a suicide is not always like it is on television. Death is a complex process, and given a choice, if I were terminally ill and believed assisted suicide to be the best alternative, I would want an experienced and compassionate physician to do the assisting.

○ *How do people who assist in a suicide react?*

Although the ways in which people react depend upon the circumstances of the assisted suicide, Russel Ogden found that in general, among the people he spoke with there were no regrets about helping a loved one die. "They believe what they've done is the right thing. They see it as an act of love. What comes through is the profound intimacy that they've experienced. Some even said it was an extraordinary privilege to be invited by the patient to help them with their death." Ogden added, however, that there were regrets over how the experience unfolded, "particularly with the botched cases."

Often the biggest burden carried by those who participate in an assisted suicide is having to remain silent about what they've been through. And for some people, there's guilt over having broken the law. Some people may also experience a sense of guilt over having "killed" a loved one. I spoke with one young woman who helped her terminally ill mother die by giving her a fatal dose of morphine. This was something they had discussed many times. Her mother couldn't have been more clear about her desire to die. But still, the daughter said, "I can't shake the feeling that I killed my mother. I know this is what she wanted, and she would have died in a few days or weeks anyway, and it was such a relief when she was finally at peace. But *I* did it. *I* was the one who gave her the drugs that made her stop breathing."

The emotion I remember most clearly as things unfolded with my friend was fear. I was scared that we'd only make things worse. And I was scared that we'd get caught. Though my friend and his wife ultimately decided that I should remain on the sidelines so that I would be spared any danger of being implicated should the truth come out, I was still close enough to what was going on to feel like I was holding my breath, from that first conversation at his bedside, to trying to get a doctor to prescribe enough drugs to do the job, to filling the prescription, giving him the drugs, and then waiting and waiting.

I wasn't there when he took the medication or when he died, but when the call came, I was filled with a sense of relief that it was over, and then almost immediately I was overcome by profound grief. We had done what he had asked us to do. He had died in the way he wanted—even though it took a little longer than expected. But he was gone, and that realization brought with it all the pain and anguish one would expect with the loss of a beloved friend.

○ *Who is Dr. Jack Kevorkian?*

Dr. Jack Kevorkian, a pathologist by training, is the person most visibly identified with the battle over the legalization of assisted suicide. Kevorkian first gained national attention in 1990 when he used his invention, the "suicide machine," to help a fifty-four-year-old woman with Alzheimer's disease take her own life. The machine allowed the woman to press a button that released a fatal combination of drugs intravenously into her system. She was dead within minutes.

Since 1990, Kevorkian has challenged local authorities by very publicly helping at least twenty-five people take their lives, although he no longer uses the "suicide machine." He has stated time and again that his goal in each suicide has been to help end the person's suffering. Kevorkian has stood trial on several occasions, but he has never been convicted.

Some people call Kevorkian's efforts heroic and consider him a champion for the cause of assisted suicide. Others see him as an irresponsible headline grabber who has distorted the current debate and deflected attention from the broader issue of how to deal compassionately with people at the end of their lives.

○ *What are the major organizations that offer information to those interested in assisted suicide?*

There are several organizations in the United States concerned with assisted suicide that provide information to the public. For information on three of these organizations, please see the appendix.

○ *Are there any organizations that provide general information on end-of-life issues other than assisted suicide?*

Assisted suicide is only part of the larger issue of how we deal with the end of life, and there are many places to get information on everything from living wills to choosing whether to die in a hospital or at home. You can ask your doctor to recommend a local organization or talk to a social worker at the hospital where you or a your loved one is being treated.

One organization I recommend is Choice in Dying, a national not-for-profit group "dedicated to serving the needs of dying patients and their families." For more information on this organization, please see the appendix.

○ *What books do you recommend reading to learn more about issues concerning the end of life and assisted suicide?*

Please see the appendix for a list of recommended books on this topic.

APPENDIX

Resources

General Organizations

American Association of Suicidology
4201 Connecticut Avenue, NW, Suite 310
Washington, DC 20008
Tel: 202-237-2280
Fax: 202-237-2282
E-mail: mcdo117w@wonder.em.cdc.gov

The American Association of Suicidology is a national organization dedicated to research, prevention, and education about suicide. The AAS also certifies crisis workers as well as suicide-prevention and crisis-intervention centers. The organization's membership is made up of both individuals and groups with an interest in suicide. The AAS holds three major conferences a year and publishes a quarterly journal as well as two newsletters: *NewsLink,* a publication sent to all members; and *Surviving Suicide,* for survivors and support groups for survivors. The AAS also provides referrals to local support groups for survivors of suicide.

> American Suicide Foundation
> 1045 Park Avenue, Suite 3C
> New York, NY 10028
> Tel: 212-410-1111
> Fax: 212-410-0352

The American Suicide Foundation supports research, education, and treatment programs with the goal of preventing suicide. The ASF also publishes a seasonal newsletter for those concerned about suicide and those who have lost a loved one to suicide. On request, the foundation will provide informational material, including listings of local support groups for survivors of suicide.

End-of-Life Decisions

For information on end-of-life issues other than assisted suicide, from living wills to choosing whether to die in a hospital or at home, I recommend contacting:

> Choice in Dying
> 200 Varick Street, 10th floor
> New York, NY 10014-4810
> Tel: 212-366-5540 and 800-989-WILL (9455)
> Fax: 212-366-5337

Choice in Dying is a national not-for-profit group "dedicated to serving the needs of dying patients and their families." The organization developed the first living will twenty-five years ago and is the nation's largest provider of free, state-specific advance directives. *Advance directives* is the general term used for two types of legal documents: the living will, and the durable power of attorney for health care. Living wills allow individuals to put into writing their wishes about medical treatment at the end of life. And durable powers of attorney for health care allow individuals to appoint someone they trust, such as a spouse, adult child, or close friend, to make medical treatment decisions in the event they cannot speak for themselves.

Choice in Dying provides a range of services, from free counseling about end-of-life issues to public education through a national network of volunteer speakers. The organization also provides on request a variety of publications that can help answer questions.

Assisted Suicide/End of Life Decisions

The following three organizations support the right of people to choose how to deal with the end of their lives. The fact that I have listed these organizations does not mean I endorse their work.

Compassion in Dying
P.O. Box 75295
Seattle, WA 98125
Tel: 206-624-2775
Fax: 206-624-2673

Compassion in Dying is a nonprofit charitable organization, staffed primarily by volunteers, that offers counseling, information, and emotional support to terminally ill people who are seeking to hasten the end of their lives.

According to the Reverend Ralph Mero, its executive director, Compassion in Dying is the only organization in the United States that provides actual assistance to terminally ill people who wish to end their lives. The organization has strict guidelines and safeguards, so that only those it deems both mentally competent and terminally ill will be helped.

ERGO!
24829 Norris Lane
Junction City, OR 97448
Tel: 503-998-3285
Fax: 503-998-1873

ERGO! (Euthanasia Research and Guidance Organization) "is not directly connected with changing the law but with ensuring that the forthcoming law is carried out humanely and fairly and that dying people have the availability—as a right— to aid-in-dying from a willing physician."

The president of ERGO! is Derek Humphry, who is also a cofounder of the Hemlock Society and the author of *Final Exit*. (Humphry is a controversial figure among the proponents of legalized doctor-assisted suicide.)

Hemlock Society USA
P.O. Box 11830
Eugene, OR 97440
Tel: 800-247-7421

The Hemlock Society USA is a nonprofit organization with eighty-five member organizations in thirty-nine states and forty thousand members in the United States and abroad. It was founded in 1980 in Los Angeles.

According to its mission statement, the Hemlock Society USA believes that "terminally ill people should have the right to self-determination for all end of life decisions. Because Hemlock reveres life, dying people must be able to retain their dignity, integrity, and self-respect. We encourage, through a program of education and research, public acceptance of voluntary physician aid in dying for the terminally ill."

The Hemlock Society USA and its local member organizations sponsor conferences, meetings, and various publications.

Sexual-Minority Youth (Gay, Lesbian, etc.)

Hetrick-Martin Institute
2 Astor Place
New York, NY 10003
Tel: 212-674-2400 and
    212-674-8695 (TDD; hearing impaired)
Fax: 212-674-8650

Hetrick-Martin has professionally trained staff counselors who can talk by phone and/or provide referrals to local resources for sexual-minority youth.

Suicide/Crisis Hot Lines

There are literally hundreds of suicide/crisis telephone lines across the country (which you can find by checking the front section of your local telephone book under "Suicide" or "Crisis"). Rather than list all of them, I've generally listed telephone lines that are certified by the American Association of Suicidology or are simply members of that organization. (If a line is certified, it means that the organization that runs the line has applied for certification and has met operational guidelines set by the AAS.) For selected major cities where there are no certified or membership lines, I've listed one of the unaffiliated suicide/crisis lines. All the lines listed are operational twenty-four hours a day, unless otherwise noted. All toll-free 800 numbers are for in-state calls only, unless otherwise noted.

○ ○ ○

(# = certified by the AAS)
(* = member of the AAS)

Alabama

○ Auburn
Crisis Center of East Alabama*
205-821-8600
8 A.M. to midnight Sunday through Thursday; twenty-four
    hours Friday and Saturday.

○ Birmingham
Crisis Center#
205-323-7777

○ Mobile
Contact Mobile*
205-431-5111

Alaska

○ Anchorage
Alaska Crisis Line, Inc.*
907-276-1600 and 800-478-1600

○ Fairbanks
  Fairbanks Crisis Line*
  907-452-4357

Arizona

○ Phoenix
  Phoenix South Crisis Services*
  602-271-0695

○ Tempe
  EMPACT Suicide Prevention Center#
  602-784-1500

Arkansas

○ Springdale
  Northeast Arkansas Crisis Center*
  501-756-2337 and 800-640-2680

California

○ Alameda County
  Suicide Prevention Crisis Intervention of Alameda
      County#
  510-849-2212

○ Los Angeles
  Los Angeles Suicide Prevention Center#
  213-381-5111

○ Monterey County
  Suicide Prevention and Crisis Center of Monterey
      County#

408-649-8008 (Monterey)
408-424-0902 (Salinas)

o Sacramento
Sacramento Suicide Prevention Crisis Line*
916-368-3111

o San Diego
County of San Diego CRISIS Team#
619-236-3339 and 800-479-3339 (San Diego County only)

o San Francisco
San Francisco Suicide Prevention Center#
415-781-0500

o San Jose
Santa Clara County Suicide and Crisis Service#
408-279-3312

o San Mateo County
Crisis Intervention and Suicide Prevention Center of San
Mateo County#
415-692-6655

Colorado

o Denver
Suicide and Crisis Control
303-757-0988

o Fort Collins
Crisis and Information Helpline of Larimer County*
303-229-0888

○ Greeley
  Weld County Suicide Prevention Coalition*
  303-353-3686

○ Pueblo
  Pueblo Suicide Prevention Center#
  719-544-1133

Connecticut

○ Hartford
  The Samaritans of the Capital Region*
  203-232-2121

○ Norwalk
  InfoLine of Southwestern Connecticut#
  203-853-2525 and 800-203-1234

○ Plainville
  Wheeler Clinic Emergency Services Crisis Line#
  203-747-6801

Delaware

○ Milford
  Kent/Sussex Mobile Crisis Unit*
  800-345-6785

○ Wilmington
  Crisis Intervention Center New Castle County Mental
    Health Center
  302-577-2484 and 800-652-2929

District of Columbia

o Washington
Samaritans of Washington DC, Inc.
202-362-8100

Florida

o Gainesville
Alachua County Crisis Center#
904-376-4444

o Miami
Switchboard of Miami, Inc.#
305-358-4357

o Pinellas Park
Personal Enrichment Through Mental Health Services
   (MHS)#
813-791-3131

o Rockledge
Crisis Services of Brevard County, Inc.#
407-631-8944

o Tampa
Hillsborough City Crisis Center, Inc.#
813-238-8821

Georgia

o Atlanta
Emergency Mental Health Services
404-730-1600

Hawaii

○ Honolulu
Helping Hands Hawaii#
808-521-4555

Idaho

○ Boise
Emergency Crisis Line
208-334-0808

Illinois

○ Aurora
Crisis Line of the Fox Valley#
708-897-5522

○ Bloomington
PATH, Personal Assistance Telephone Help#
309-827-4005

○ Chicago
Affiliated Psychologist Ltd. Crisis Line*
312-286-3100

○ Edgemont
Call For Help, Suicide and Crisis Intervention#
618-397-0963

○ Joliet
Crisis Line of Will County#
815-722-3344

○ Wood River
Crisis Services of Madison County#
618-251-4073

Indiana

○ Indianapolis
Mental Health Association in Marion County*
317-251-7575

Iowa

○ Cedar Rapids
Foundation II, Inc.#
319-362-2174

○ Des Moines
Community Telephone Service Crisis Line*
515-244-1000

Kansas

○ Lawrence
Headquarters, Inc.*
913-841-2345

○ Wichita
Sedgwick County Department of Mental Health*
316-686-7465

Kentucky

○ Louisville
Crisis and Information Center#
502-589-4313

Louisiana

○ Baton Rouge
Baton Rouge Crisis Intervention Center, Inc.#
504-924-3900

○ New Orleans
Volunteer and Information Agency#
504-523-2673

Maine

○ Skowhegan
Crisis Stabilization Unit of Somerset County#
207-474-2506, 8 A.M. to 10 P.M.
800-452-1933, twenty-four hours (Somerset County only)

Maryland

○ Baltimore
First Step Youth Services Center*
410-521-3800

○ Columbia
Grassroots Crisis Intervention Center, Inc.#
410-531-6677

○ Lenham
Prince George's County Hotline and Suicide Prevention
Center#
301-731-0004

○ Rockville
Montgomery County Hotline#
301-738-2255

Massachusetts

o Boston
  The Samaritans#
  617-247-0220

o New Bedford
  New Bedford Crisis Center#
  508-996-3154

Michigan

o Detroit
  NSO Emergency Telephone Service/Suicide Prevention
    Center#
  313-224-7000

o Kalamazoo
  Gryphon Place#
  616-381-4357

o Royal Oak
  Common Ground/Royal Oak#
  810-543-2900

o Traverse City
  Third Level Crisis Intervention, Inc.#
  616-922-4800

Minnesota

o Minneapolis
  Crisis Connection#
  612-379-6388

Mississippi

o Columbus
  Contact Helpline
  601-328-0200

Missouri

o St. Louis
  Life Crisis Services, Inc.#
  314-647-4357

Montana

o Kalispell
  Help Net, First Call for Help, Inc.
  800-332-8425

Nebraska

o Boys Town
  Father Flanagan's Boys' Home*
  800-448-3000 (national hot line)
  800-448-1833 (TDD; hearing-impaired, national hot line)

o Lincoln
  Personal Crisis Service
  402-475-5171

Nevada

o Reno
  Suicide Prevention and Crisis Call Center#
  702-323-6111

New Hampshire

o Concord
Emergency Services /CNHCMHS, Inc.#
800-852-3388

o Lebanon
Headrest, Inc.#
603-448-4400

o Manchester
Health Center of Greater Manchester#
603-668-4111
Twenty-four-hour answering service

o Salem
Center for Life Management#
603-893-3548, 9 A.M. to 5 P.M.
603-432-2253, 5 P.M. to 9 A.M.

New Jersey

o Moorestown
Contact Burlington County*
609-234-8888

o Newark
Emergency Psychiatric Services
201-623-2323

New Mexico

o Albuquerque
Crisis Unit Bernalillo Mental Health Clinic
505-843-2800

New York

○ Albany
  Samaritans of the Capital District*
  518-463-2323

○ Buffalo
  Suicide Prevention and Crisis Service, Inc.#
  716-834-3131

○ Ithaca
  Suicide Prevention and Crisis Service of Tomkins
      County#
  607-272-1616

○ New York City
  The Samaritans
  212-673-3000

○ Poughkeepsie
  Duchess County Department of Mental Hygiene
      Crisis Line#
  914-485-9700

North Carolina

○ Burlington
  Suicide and Crisis Service/Alamance County#
  910-227-6220

○ Charlotte
  Reachline Telephone Crisis Counseling
      Services*
  704-333-6121

North Dakota

○ Fargo
  HotLine#
  800-472-2911

Ohio

○ Akron
  Portage Path Support Hotline#
  216-434-1214

○ Canton
  Crisis Intervention Center of Stark County#
  216-452-6000

○ Cleveland
  St. Vincent Charity Hospital Psychiatric Emergency
    Services Crisis Line#
  216-229-2211

○ Dayton
  Suicide Prevention Center, Inc.#
  513-297-4777

○ Delaware
  Help Anonymous, Inc.#
  614-369-3316

○ Mt. Gilead
  Hope Line, Inc.#
  419-947-2520

○ Oxford
  Oxford Crisis and Referral Center*
  513-523-4146 and 800-523-4146

- Youngstown
  Help Hotline Crisis Center, Inc.#
  216-747-2696

Oklahoma

- Oklahoma City
  Contact Helpline
  405-848-2273

Oregon

- Portland
  Metro Crisis Intervention Service#
  503-223-6161

Pennsylvania

- Harrisburg
  Dauphin County Crisis Intervention*
  717-232-7511

- Philadelphia
  Philadelphia Suicide and Crisis Center
  215-686-4420

- Pittsburgh
  Contact Pittsburgh, Inc.#
  412-782-4023

Rhode Island

- Providence
  The Samaritans of Rhode Island*
  401-272-4044 and 800-365-4044

South Carolina

○ Greenville
Crisisline*
803-271-8888

○ North Charleston
Hotline
803-744-4357 and 800-922-2283
Tri-County Area TeenLine (for young people in 6th to 12th
    grades)
803-747-TEEN
800-273-TALK (Tri-County area only)

South Dakota

○ Sioux Falls
Crisisline Volunteer and Information Center
605-339-4357

Tennessee

○ Knoxville
Mobile Crisis Unit*
615-637-6100

○ Nashville
Crisis Intervention Center, Inc.#
615-244-7444

Texas

○ Amarillo
Suicide and Crisis Center#
806-359-6699

○ Dallas
  Contact#
  214-233-2233
  Suicide and Crisis Center#
  214-828-1000

○ Fort Worth
  Crisis Intervention /Family Service, Inc.#
  817-927-5544 and 817-827-5545

○ Houston
  Crisis Intervention of Houston, Inc.#
  713-228-1505 (English)
  713-526-8088 (Spanish)

○ Plano
  Crisis Center of Collin County#
  214-881-0088

Utah

○ Salt Lake City
  Salt Lake Mental Health*
  801-483-5444

Vermont

○ Brattleboro
  Hotline for Help, Inc.
  800-639-8036 (Maine, New Hampshire, and Vermont only)

Virginia

○ Arlington
  Northern Virginia Hotline#
  703-527-4077

○ Portsmouth
Suicide Crisis Center, Inc.#
804-399-6393

Washington

○ Seattle
Crisis Clinic of King County#
206-461-3222 and 800-244-5767
800-461-3219 (TDD; hearing-impaired)

West Virginia

○ Charleston
Contact Kanawha Valley
304-346-0826

○ Wheeling
Upper Ohio Valley Crisis Hotline
304-234-8161

Wisconsin

○ Green Bay
Crisis Center of Family Service Association*
414-436-8888

○ Madison
Emergency Services Mental Health Center of Dane
County*
608-251-2345

○ Milwaukee
  Helpline
  414-271-3123

Wyoming

○ Cheyenne
  Cheyenne Helpline
  307-634-4469

SELECTED
BIBLIOGRAPHY

Assisted Suicide

Ahronheim, Dr. Judith, and Doron Weber. *Final Passages: Positive Choices for the Dying and Their Loved Ones.* New York: Simon & Schuster, 1992.

Callahan, Daniel. *The Troubled Dream of Life.* New York: Simon & Schuster, 1993.

Humphry, Derek. *Final Exit.* Portland, OR: Hemlock Society, 1991.

Quill, Timothy E., M.D. *Death and Dignity: Making Choices and Taking Charge.* New York: W. W. Norton & Company, 1993.

Rollin, Betty. *Last Wish*. New York: Linden Press/Simon & Schuster, 1985.

I also recommend the chapter on euthanasia and assisted suicide in the 1995 edition of Herbert Hendin's book *Suicide in America* (listed below under "General" books) and a novel, *A Stone Boat*, by Andrew Solomon (Winchester, MA: Faber & Faber, 1994). Basing the main character on his mother, Solomon tells the story of a woman who takes her life at the end of a terminal illness. I also strongly recommend Solomon's superb article on his mother and euthanasia/assisted suicide; titled "A Death of One's Own," it was published in the May 22, 1995, issue of the *New Yorker*.

Clinical Books

Hatton, Corrine Loing, and Sharon McBride Valente, eds. *Suicide: Assessment and Intervention*. Norwalk, CT: Appleton-Century-Crofts, 1984.

Jacobs, Douglas, ed. *Suicide and Clinical Practice*. Washington, DC: American Psychiatric Press, 1992.

Lester, David. *Why People Kill Themselves: A 1980s Summary of Research on Suicidal Behavior*. Springfield, IL: Charles C. Thomas, 1983.

Coping with Suicide/Suicide Survivors

Bolton, Iris. *My Son, My Son: A Guide to Healing After a Suicide in the Family*. Atlanta: Bolton Press, 1983.

Cain, Albert C., ed. *Survivors of Suicide*. Springfield, IL: Charles C. Thomas, 1972.

Hammer, Signe. *By Her Own Hand.* New York: Vintage Books/Random House, 1992.

Hewett, John H. *After Suicide.* Philadelphia: Westminster Press, 1980.

Kuklin, Susan. *After a Suicide: Young People Speak Up.* New York: G. P. Putnam's Sons, 1994.

Lukas, Christopher, and Henry M. Seiden, Ph.D. *Silent Grief: Living in the Wake of Suicide.* New York: Charles Scribner's Sons, 1987.

Robinson, Rita. *Survivors of Suicide.* Van Nuys, CA: Newcastle Publishing Co., 1989.

Rosenfield, Linda. *Left Alive: After a Suicide Death in the Family.* Springfield, IL: Charles C. Thomas, 1984.

Smolin, Ann, and John Guinan. *Healing After the Suicide of a Loved One.* New York: Fireside/Simon & Schuster, 1993.

Gay and Lesbian

Remafedi, Dr. Gary, ed. *Death by Denial: Studies of Suicide in Gay and Lesbian Teenagers.* Boston: Alyson Publications, 1994.

Rofes, Eric E. *"I Thought People Like That Killed Themselves": Lesbians, Gay Men and Suicide.* San Francisco: Grey Fox Press, 1983.

General

Colt, George Howe. *The Enigma of Suicide.* New York: Touchstone/Simon & Schuster, 1993.

Farberow, Norman L., ed. *Suicide in Different Cultures*. Baltimore: University Park Press, 1975.

Farberow, Norman L., and Edwin S. Shneidman, eds. *The Cry for Help*. New York: McGraw-Hill, 1965.

Heckler, Richard A. *Waking Up Alive: The Descent, the Suicide Attempt and the Return to Life*. New York: Grosset/ Putnam, 1994.

Hendin, Herbert, M.D. *Suicide in America*. New York: W. W. Norton & Company, 1995 [originally 1982].

Lester, David. *Questions and Answers About Suicide*. Springfield, IL: Charles C. Thomas, 1987.

Nuland, Sherwin B. *How We Die: Reflections on Life's Final Chapter*. New York: Alfred A. Knopf, 1994.

Quinnett, Paul G. *Suicide: The Forever Decision*. New York: Crossroad Publishing Company, 1993.

Shneidman, Edwin S., and Norman L. Farberow. *Clues to Suicide*. New York: McGraw-Hill, 1957.

Stengel, Edwin. *Suicide and Attempted Suicide*. New York: Jason Aronson, 1974.

Historical Works

Donne, John. *Biathanatos*. New York: Arno Press, 1977.

Durkheim, Emile. *Suicide*. Translated by John Spaulding and George Simson. New York: Free Press, 1951.

Literature

Alvarez, A. *The Savage God*. New York: Bantam Books, 1973.

Goethe, Johann Wolfgang von. *The Sorrows of Young Werther*. Translated by Elizabeth Mayer and Louise Bogan. New York: Vintage Books, 1973.

Middlebrook, Diane Wood. *Anne Sexton: A Biography*. New York: Vintage Books/Random House, 1992.

Miller, John, ed. *On Suicide*. San Francisco: Chronicle Books, 1992.

Plath, Sylvia. *The Bell Jar*. New York: Bantam Books, 1972.

Styron, William. *Darkness Visible*. New York: Vintage Books/Random House, 1990.

Teen/Youth Suicide

Aarons, Leroy. *Prayers for Bobby: A Mother's Coming to Terms with the Suicide of Her Gay Son*. San Francisco: HarperSanFrancisco, 1995.

Klagsbrun, Francine. *Too Young to Die: Youth and Suicide*. Boston: Houghton Mifflin, 1976.

Kuklin, Susan. *After a Suicide: Young People Speak Up*. New York: G. P. Putnam's Sons, 1994.

Leder, Jane Mersky. *Dead Serious: A Book for Teenagers About Suicide*. New York: Atheneum, 1987.

Besides these nonfiction books, I recommend a young-adult novel by Richard Peck called *Remembering the Good Times* (New York: Delacorte, 1985).

INDEX

Abandonment, 122

Advance directives, 205

Aftermath of suicide: anger, 122–24; blame, 125–27; body identification, 155–56; coming to terms with suicide, 157–59; compassion, 130–31; confusion, 128–29; denial, 119–21; depression, 132–33; fear, 133–34; grief, 121–22; guilt, 124–25; isolation, 132; rejection/abandonment, 122; relief, 129–30; self-recrimination, 127–28; shame/embarrassment, 131–32; shock, 118–19; suicidal feelings, 133; support/help during, 159–64, 166; to finding body, 154–55; of youth suicide, 149–50. *See also* Survivors of suicide

Age factors, 16, 52

AIDS, 19–20; and assisted suicide, 195–97

Alcohol, 42–43, 69

Alcoholism, 31

Alm, Jeff, 35, 43

Alterman, Marsha, 64

Alvarez, A., 22, 27

American Association of Suicidology, 111, 166, 203–4

American Suicide Foundation, 204

Anger, 122–24

Meyer, Eve R., 52, 56, 113
Meyer, William F., III, 179–82
Morrish, Donna, 161–62
Motives for suicide: for attempts,
   93; clues from notes, 38–39; for
   community/cause, 32–34; for
   the elderly, 78–80; haunting
   legacy of, 29–30; psychologi-
   cal/physiological, 30–32; sudden loss/trauma/threat as,
   35–37; of young children,
   39–40; in youth suicide, 64–67
Motto, Jerome, 25
Myths about suicide, 10–11

National Suicide Prevention
   Week, 111
Negative reactions, 150–54
Netherlands, 191–92
NewsLink (AAS newsletter), 204
Nuland, Sherwin B., 50–51, 56,
   192

O'Barry, Richard, 12
O'Connor, Wendy, 124
Official denial, 120. See also De-
   nial
Ogden, Russel D., 188–89, 195–98
Okouchi, Kiyoteru, 37
Oregon assisted-suicide law,
   187–89
Outside threat motive, 36–37

Personality disorder, 31

Physical infirmity, 31
Physician-assisted suicide. See
   Doctor-assisted suicide
Planning suicide, 11–12
Plotkin, Daniel A., 87
Police officers, 20–21
Political factors: in suicide
   method, 55; in suicide motive,
   33–34
Preston, Thomas A., 177
Professions, 20–22
Psychological/physiological fac-
   tors: in suicide methods, 53–54;
   in suicide motives, 30–32
Punishment motive, 31–32

Quang Duc, 55
"Quest for Evolutionary Meaning
   in the Persistence of Suicide"
   (article), 33
Quill, Timothy E., 189–90
Quinlan, Karen Ann, 171–72
Quinnett, Paul G., 42–43, 92

Racial factors, 16–18
Refusing medical treatment, 2
Rejection, suicide as, 122
Relief about loved one's suicide,
   129–30
Religious issues, 7–9, 186
Revenge motive, 31–32
Right to die issue, 171–72
Robinson, Rita, 7, 10, 108
Rock music, 69

Suicide risk: during depression treatment, 41–42; for elderly, 82–85, 88; professional assessment of, 109; response to, 110–11; of surviving families, 156–57; for youth suicide, 67–69. *See also* Warning signs

Suicidology, 13

Support groups: during suicide aftermath, 159–64; hot lines as, 112–14; locating/contacting, 166; for terminally ill, 204–7

Surviving Suicide (AAS newsletter), 204

Survivors of suicide: children (adult) as, 144–48; children (young) as, 141–44; coming to terms with suicide by, 157–64; constructive/negative reactions to, 150–53, 164–65; described, 165; identification of body by, 155–56; locating support groups for, 166; parents as, 139–41; siblings as, 148–49; spouse as, 137–39; suicide risk for, 156–57; who have found suicide victim, 154–55. *See also* Aftermath of suicide

Survivors of Suicide (Robinson), 7, 10, 108

Suttee, 34

Teen suicide, 60. *See also* Youth suicide

Terminal illness: assisted suicide for, 172–75, 183–87; defining, 188; Measure 16 on, 187–89; support groups for, 204–7

Therapy: for coping with suicide, 161–63; risk during depression, 41–42

Touched with Fire: Manic-Depressive Illness and the Artistic Temperament (Jamison), 21

Trauma motive, 35–37

Treatments: availability of, 102; for suicidal feelings, 103–4

Underreporting suicide, 3

Verbal clues, 107

Volcano leaping, 46

Voluntary euthanasia, 170

Voluntary Euthanasia Society of London, 176

Warning signs: for elderly suicide, 83–84, 110; listed, 108–9; myths on, 10; for youth suicide, 68–69, 110. *See also* Suicide risk

White males, 14–15, 83

World Federation of the Right to Die Societies, 191

Writers, 21–22

Youth suicide: demographics on, 63–64; high rate of, 59–63;